ISLAM
AND
TERRORISM

REVISED AND UPDATED EDITION

ISLAM
AND
TERRORISM

REVISED AND UPDATED EDITION

MARK A. GABRIEL, PhD

Most CHARISMA HOUSE BOOK GROUP products are available at special quantity discounts for bulk purchase for sales promotions, premiums, fund-raising, and educational needs. For details, write Charisma House Book Group, 600 Rinehart Road, Lake Mary, Florida 32746, or telephone (407) 333-0600.

ISLAM AND TERRORISM REVISED AND UPDATED
by Mark A. Gabriel, PhD
Published by FrontLine
Charisma Media/Charisma House Book Group
600 Rinehart Road
Lake Mary, Florida 32746
www.charismahouse.com

Scripture quotations are from the Holy Bible, New International Version®, NIV®. Copyright © 1973, 1978, 1984, 2011 by Biblica, Inc.™ Used by permission of Zondervan. All rights reserved worldwide. www.zondervan .com The "NIV" and "New International Version" are trademarks registered in the United States Patent and Trademark Office by Biblica, Inc.™

Quotations from the Quran marked "Ali translation" are from *The Quran Translation*, 7th edition, by Abdullah Yusef Ali (Elmhurst, NY: Tahrike Tarsile Quran, Inc., 2001).

Quotations from the Quran marked "*The Noble Quran*" are from *The Noble Quran*, English Translation of the Meanings and Commentary published by King Fahd of Saudi Arabia in Medina, "The City of Light," Saudi Arabia in 1998. The translators were Dr. Muhammad Taqi-ud-Din Al-Hilali and Dr. Muhammad Muhsin Khan.

Copyright © 2002, 2015 by Mark A. Gabriel, PhD
All rights reserved

Cover design by Vincent Pirozzi
Design Director: Justin Evans

Library of Congress Control Number: 2015945093
International Standard Book Number: 978-1-62998-668-5
E-book ISBN: 978-1-62998-687-6

While the author has made every effort to provide accurate Internet addresses at the time of publication, neither the publisher nor the author assumes any responsibility for errors or for changes that occur after publication.

15 16 17 18 19 — 987654321
Printed in the United States of America

CONTENTS

Section II:
The Roots of Terrorism in Islam

Section IV:
The Development of Modern Jihad

Section V:
The Future of the Muslim World

PREFACE

IN THIS SECOND edition of *Islam and Terrorism* I want to bring you, my dear readers, answers to the primary questions people are asking today about violence in the name of Islam: "Where does this violence come from?" and "What has inspired this global movement of angry men and women to leave everything behind and take up arms—fighting, killing, destroying in the name of Allah?"

This edition will help you to understand the historical and the current roots that are contributing to this chaos our world is controlled by. In the end you will find ideas for the most important questions: What is the solution? Is there any solution at all? Is there any hope for peace to be established in the Middle East? With the pages of this book I try to provide the dimension of understanding that is difficult to find in the world of secular and politically correct media.

In this book I will introduce you to teachings that are widely taught throughout the Islamic world because these are the teachings from Al-Azhar University, the most influential university in the Muslim world. In order to grasp the position and influence of Al-Azhar, we can say that for Muslims it is what the Vatican is for Catholics. It can be considered the brain/educational center of Islam. So the teaching presented in this book is the Islamic teaching according to the world's leading Islamic scholars.

MY STORY

You may wonder how I can be so confident that I understand the mind-set of the radical Muslim. The reason is that with my background, I could have become one of those radicals. I grew up in a conservative Muslim household in Egypt. I started memorizing the Quran at the age of five and finished when I was twelve years old. I went on to earn a doctorate degree from the famous Al-Azhar University and was given a teaching position. I had several friends and students in my classes who were active in jihad. Personally I preferred to focus on the peaceful side of Islam, but I was unable to ignore the violent side I saw in the Quran and Islamic history. This inner struggle ultimately led me to question the basis of my faith, for which I was arrested and tortured by the Egyptian secret police.

Another important part of my story is that I am no longer a follower of Islam. This allows me to speak more freely about the teachings of Islam, but it also puts me at risk of punishment from the radicals. I have been stabbed, shot at, and threatened multiple times. I used to even receive death threats in reviews of my book that were posted online.

These issues are a fact of life for me and many others like me who have exercised their freedom of religion and have faced judgment from the Muslim world.

However, I want to make it very clear that Muslims are not my enemies, and this book does not want to talk bad about Muslims in any way. My family in Egypt and all my friends I had to leave behind when I left Islam are still Muslims. I still love them, despite all that I have gone through, and my heart is crying out for all those sincere people who are working hard during all their lives trying to do good, hoping that at the end of their lives Allah might admit them to Paradise. My heart cries out for them because I know about the sufferings that the teachings of Islam can cause. And most Muslims are born into this religion. It was not their choice. I grew up as one of them, memorizing the Quran as a child and studying Islam for many years. I know about the sufferings, the discrimination, and the lack of freedom that the teaching of Islam are causing—not only to non-Muslims but first of all to the Muslims themselves.

When you read about the very challenging teachings of Islam that bring so much pain and violence to this world, please keep in mind that I am not trying to make Muslims look bad. What I am trying to do is to help them and others see what motivates an Islamic radical. I am a free person, and today I am living in a free country. I can ask the hard questions about Islam, but the Muslim people I left behind cannot question their beliefs.

I want you to see this very, very important distinction: Islam is the religion. Muslims are people who are following the teachings of Islam according to many different interpretations. Muslims are also the ones suffering most from Islamic radicalism. Radical Muslims who are committed to live, die, and kill for jihad are the minority. By far the greatest majority of Muslims wish to live peaceful lives, to enjoy their family life, and they work hard to provide a good future to their children.

If you have Muslim friends, neighbors, or acquaintances, please be kind to them and treat them with respect. They are probably nice people living in a peaceful way and not wanting to cause trouble for you or anybody else. Do not treat them as your enemies. The best thing you can do is to enjoy your friendship and learn about their culture.

If you ever discuss religion with someone else, please keep a good attitude and be very sensitive. You don't want to hurt their religious feelings. It is normal that every person wants to defend his faith. It is very helpful to always keep in mind that above all we are all brothers and sisters in humanity—we are all searching for the truth.

SECTION I

THE REASONS
FOR RADICALISM

Chapter 1

HOW THE ARAB SPRING TURNED TO AN ISIS WINTER

N THIS CHAPTER I will explain how the hope of the Arab Spring resulted in a new level of Islamic extremism as radicals took advantage of a vacuum in leadership to gain new ground for their cause.

During the whole year of 2011 one major topic dominated the world media: the so-called Arab Spring. A revolution crying out for freedom and democracy was spreading over the whole Middle East like a bush fire. Dictator regimes, which had been in power for decades, were overthrown in just a few days.

On December 18, 2010, in Tunisia a young Tunisian man in an economically desperate situation committed suicide by setting fire on himself. This was the first spark that later created a big fire that covered the whole region of the Middle East, including Egypt, Libya, Syria, Yemen, and Bahrein.

As a result of this revolution:

- The Tunisian president Ben Ali fled his country, and his government was overthrown.

- Egyptian president Mubarak resigned and was put in jail and on trial along with his two sons and six top officials of his regime.

- The Libyan dictator Qaddafi was killed after a civil war with foreign military intervention, and his regime was overthrown.

- The president of Yemen, Ali Abdullah Saleh, was kicked out of his position and the power was handed over to a national unity government.

- In the kingdom of Bahrain a civil uprising took place that forced the king to do some government changes. However, the changes didn't stop the uprising.

- In Jordan, Morocco, Lebanon, Oman, Kuwait, Iraq, and Algeria protestors forced the governments to make constitutional reforms and governmental changes.

- In Syria the corrupted dictator president refused to leave his position and continued killing his own people. Consequently a civil war started which would keep burning for years.

In the same way a huge forest fire caused by just one little match, the overwhelming fire of the revolution in the Arab world was caused by one individual incident.

A fire, however, only will spread that much if the land is very dry. The region of the Arab world was exactly like a dry forest in a very hot summer. It was dried out by the heat of corruption, dictatorship, and economical distress. The region was heated by the misery, torture, and all the unjust trials against innocent people that were done by the corrupt dictator regimes. People were suffering from the lack of freedom and justice. The abuse of basic human rights by the secret services and the corrupt, vicious police departments had heated up the moods. The Arab region of the world was so dry, heated, and ready to get burned that the smallest spark could light a huge fire.

Eventually millions of people went to the streets to demonstrate for bread, freedom, and social justice. The world was just watching and could hardly believe what they saw. One dictatorship after the other was overthrown. The situation in the Middle East was turned upside down within a few weeks, and it seemed that the whole world was full of hope that finally peace and democracy would lead the way. Indeed, Egypt experienced a free democratic election for the first time in its history.

When the revolution that had started in Tunisia reached Egypt in the beginning of 2011, I was watching the news almost day and night. My heart was dancing inside me when the old regime finally stepped back. I was so happy to witness the end of this corrupted dictator regime that I myself had been suffering under. However, at the same time I had the strange feeling that this revolution, which had been started by the moderate young generation, might be hijacked and the country might be taken into an even deeper and darker kind of dictatorship and abuse of human rights than before. Before the revolution the people suffered corrupt regimes and corrupt politics. But now the people might fall under the dictatorship of the radical Islamic religious ideology, which can violate the basic human rights even more.

MUSLIM BROTHERHOOD TAKES
ADVANTAGE OF A NEW OPPORTUNITY

A few months later my concerns became reality. The revolution had been stolen from the young generation, who had started the revolution, calling for bread, freedom, and social justice. In Egypt Muslim Brotherhood and Salafists won the parliamentarian election and a new president, who was a member of Muslim Brotherhood, came to power. The new parliament was on its way to implement Islamic law step by step.

While various radical groups come and go, Muslim Brotherhood is the most mature and well-organized powerful Islamic radical movement in our modern history. It was established by the well-educated Egyptian Sheikh Hassan Al-Banna in 1928 as a result of the collapse and the fall of the Islamic Caliphate. The main purpose of the establishment of the Muslim Brotherhood was to restore Islam in the Muslim world in every single area of life— politics, social affairs, economy, education, jurisdiction, and military.

A brief review of their history will help you understand their strategy and position today. In the first years after their establishment during the 1930s and 1940s Muslim Brotherhood was very actively engaged in fighting against the Jews in Palestine. Later their focus turned to Egyptian internal affairs, and so in the 1950s they turned aggressively against all politicians whom they deemed too secular. They assassinated the Egyptian prime minister al-Nuqrashi in 1948 and later attempted to assassinate president Gamal Abdel Nasser. Their very radical behavior triggered, however, a very harsh reaction: President Nasser went after them with resoluteness. He killed many of them and put many of them in prison for many, many years. Muslim Brotherhood was officially banned for the following decades. Nevertheless, the organization continued their work underground.

When the powerful wind of change started to shake the whole Middle East during the Arab Spring and spread the hope that this revolution would bring true democracy and liberty to the Middle East, many signs very soon showed how well prepared the political ground was for Muslim Brotherhood to take power and how well prepared the organization was to jump in and use this unique opportunity. They had learned from their past and were well prepared for a better future. They changed their strategy and adapted a peaceful approach. Having the long-term goal in mind, they presented themselves as modern, peaceful, and in favor of democracy. This way they were able to gain international support and win the democratic elections. Their strategy was quite successful as previously mentioned. They won both the majority in the parliament as well as the presidential elections.

Their success, however, didn't last long, and it would soon provide justification for the new level of extremism we see in ISIS, the Islamic State in Iraq and Syria. After just a few months the democratically elected president Mohamed Morsi was kicked out of his position through a military coup under the leadership of Abdel Fattah al-Sisi, who shortly later became the new president. Many Egyptians considered this coup as a great liberation and al-Sisi was viewed by many as a messiah. And indeed, under al-Sisi the country recovered economically, and peace in the country was reestablished. However, the *way* this new government radically wiped out all its political opponents soon revealed that with this new president returned the same kind of dictatorship as before the revolution. Again all political opponents were wiped out with extreme harshness.

Egypt can be considered the heart of the Middle East. Whatever happens there has a great influence on the rest of the Middle East. This is why the development there is crucial and kind of representative for the entire Middle East.

For Muslim Brotherhood and all the other Islamic groups that had been dreaming to get rid of this kind of corrupt and secular regimes, the Egyptian backlash was a real trauma. I strongly believe that the failure of the peaceful approach of Muslim Brotherhood in Egypt has greatly contributed to the fast spread of the extremely violent group of ISIS.

How ISIS Gained Power

ISIS can be seen as the grandchild of Muslim Brotherhood. In June 2014 the militant group declared it is establishing a caliphate spanning across Iraq and Syria. The Egyptian military crushing Muslim Brotherhood after the Arab Spring gave ISIS an excuse for their extremism. They could look to Egypt and say that gaining power through politics doesn't work; peaceful change is not possible. The only way is the extreme way.

Setting up a caliphate ruled by the strict Islamic law has long been a goal of many jihadists, who complain that Islam has been taken out of society and who demand for Islam to rule again—in every area of life. They go to Islamic history and point to Muhammad's example of war—aggression and terrorism and the use of fear and terror. You will read these stories in detail in this book.

ISIS is operating under the premise that they are living

in the *house of war* and therefore must use all means at their disposal to conquer territory for their cause. The concept of *house of war* and *house of peace* has been discussed for centuries in Islamic law, and an understanding of it is essential to make sense of what is happening in the Islamic world today.

These terms do not come directly from the Quran or hadith, but the early scholars of Islam created these terms in order to describe the environment of a place where a Muslim may be living. For example, Mecca during the time of Muhammad's weakness and persecution would have been a house of war (*Dar-ul-Harb*). As a result, after he was prepared, Muhammad declared war on Mecca and established Islamic authority there. Medina, when it was governed and ruled by Muslims, would be considered a house of peace (*Dar-ul-Islam*).

Abu Hanifa, one of the founders of the four Muslim legal schools, had a moderate standard for these two terms. He said the most important issue is the security of Muslims. If Muslims are in a secure place, it is *Dar-ul-Islam*; if not, then they are in *Dar-ul-Harb*. By these standards, a nation where Islam could be practiced freely (such as the United States or England) would be considered *Dar-ul-Islam*. However, another group of Muslim scholars reject this definition. They say that *Dar-ul-Harb* is any place not ruled by Islam and not submitting to Islamic law.[1]

Sayyid Qutb popularized the strict interpretation in his most influential book, *Milestones Along the Road*. Qutb declared:

1. *Dar-ul-Islam* is that place where the Islamic state is established and *Sharia* is the highest authority and God's limits are observed and

where all the Muslims administer the affairs of the state with mutual consultation.

2. The rest of the world is the home of hostility (*Dar-ul-Harb*). A Muslim can have only two possible relations with *Dar-ul-Harb*: peace with a contractual agreement or war. A country with which there is a treaty will not be considered the home of Islam.[2]

A Muslim must only declare loyalty to *Dar-ul-Islam*, not to a particular nationality. Qutb wrote:

A Muslim has no country except that part of the earth where the Sharia of God is established....; a Muslim has no nationality except his belief...; a Muslim has no relatives except those who share the belief in God.[3]

A committed Muslim will have only one defining characteristic—his faith. All other identity not based in his faith is irrelevant, including lineage, race, nationality, and family. These relationships were from the time of ignorance before Islam, says the radical.

The Future of ISIS

ISIS has written a new powerful chapter in the story of Islamic radicalism. They have recruited twenty thousand fighters from ninety nations, including France, Morocco, Russia, Saudi Arabia, Tunisia, the United States, and Canada.[4] They have taken control of portions of Iraq's Anbar Province and oil-rich areas in Syria and are operating transnationally.[5] The United States and its allies have been carrying out air strikes against ISIS targets, and officials claim thousands of militants have been killed.[6] Even if ISIS will eventually be defeated, the world must be prepared for others who will take their place. This is because the philosophy that drives groups such as Muslim Brotherhood and ISIS needs to be understood and addressed in the Islamic world.

Chapter 2

FIVE PILLARS OF ISLAMIC RADICALISM

D ESPITE THE DIFFERENCES between radical groups, certain principles are maintained from group to group, and these principles have the strength to draw in new generations of radicals. These principles did not stay within national borders. They are exported throughout the world through cyberspace, winning more Muslim hearts and minds.

I call these guiding principles the "Five Pillars of Radical Islamic Philosophy." They are:

1. Obey no law but Islamic law.

2. Infidels are all around.

3. Islam must rule.

4. Jihad is the only way to win.

5. Faith is the reason.

I introduced these principles in my earlier book *Journey into the Mind of an Islamic Terrorist.* If you can grasp these five principles, you will have an excellent understanding of the mind-set of any Islamic radical who is basing his fight on his religion, not politics.

PILLAR 1: NO LAW BUT ISLAMIC LAW

There is one point that separates the radical Muslim from all others: Islamic law. Since the beginning of the revival of modern Islamic terrorism, the radical leaders have been crying out for their governments to implement Islamic law.

Islamic law is the line that divides the religious terrorist from the secular terrorist. I have listed it as Pillar 1 because without it, the radicals would have no reason to condemn secular governments and declare jihad.

Islamic law is an incredibly powerful concept because it is viewed as a direct command from Allah. Even more so, the radical scholars attached it inseparably to the worship of Allah.

How did Islamic law develop? And who is living by Islamic law today? Islamic law began with Muhammad settling disputes in the new Muslim political state. When issues arose, he would either receive a revelation from Allah or he would make his own judgment. For example, after military conquests, the people asked Muhammad how to divide the spoils of war, and in response, Muhammad declared that he had received a revelation from Allah about the appropriate way to divide the spoils (see Surah 8.1). Once the new revelation had been announced, Muslims were required to accept his judgment.

PILLAR 2: INFIDELS ARE ALL AROUND

The radical sees himself as surrounded by infidels who are hostile to him and his message of faith. In their writings radicals put great energy into arguing that nearly all societies are infidel—both those who call themselves Muslims and the others.

Islam means submission, and to be a Muslim you must submit to Islamic law, the radicals say. They repeatedly appeal to this Quranic verse:

But no, by your Lord, they can have no Faith, until they make you (O Muhammad) judge in all disputes between them, and find in themselves no resistance against your decisions, and accept (them) with full submission.

—SURAH 4:65 (SEE ALSO SURAH 5:44 AND 3:32)

Radicals use these verses to sweepingly condemn nearly the whole world as infidel.

The radicals see Islam as an all-or-nothing faith. An individual must follow all of the regulations of Islam (according to the radical's understanding), or that person is an infidel. You cannot accept some and reject some. For example, during Muhammad's time a group of new Muslim converts wanted to keep charging interest (*usury*) for loans, even though the Quran prohibited it. At this point Muhammad received the following revelation from Allah: "The Exalted said 'O ye who believe! Fear Allah, and give up what remains of your demand for usury, if ye are indeed believers. If ye do it not, Take notice of war from Allah and His Messenger'" (Surah 2:278).

In other words, Allah required Muhammad to go to war against those who would not give up *usury* (charging interest), even though they were following other teachings of Islam. This is known in Islamic teaching as "accepting some, rejecting some." The Quran says:

Surely those who disbelieve in Allah and His apostles and (those who) desire to make a distinction between Allah and His apostles and say: We believe in some and disbelieve in others, and desire to take a course between (this and) that. These it is that are

truly the unbelievers, and we have prepared for the
unbelievers a disgraceful chastisement.
—SURAH 4:150–151, SHAKIR TRANSLATION

Another example of this philosophy is when Abu Bakr
took charge after Muhammad's death, a group of new
Muslim converts refused to continue to pay the tax to the
Islamic state. Abu Bakr sent his best general to fight them,
and he killed eighty thousand people in three bloody
months. Because Abu Bakr was the closest companion to
Muhammad, this proves to the radicals that there must be
no tolerance of partial obedience.

In conclusion, the radical is convinced that he is surrounded by infidels who must be fought to preserve Islam.
His ultimate goal is to restore the caliphate: "Islam must
rule." This is the focus of the third pillar, which you will
read next.

PILLAR 3: ISLAM MUST RULE

Westerners see the news about bombings and terrorism in
Muslim nations and in the West. Many times they throw
up their hands in frustration and ask, "What do these
people want? What are they trying to get?"

The answer is this: these terrorists want the caliphate
back, and they ultimately want Islam to rule the entire
world.

Muslims in general are very proud of the history of the
caliphate in Islam. For thirteen centuries the caliphate
united Muslim lands both spiritually and politically.

Turkey's action to end the caliphate in 1924 caused great
emotional pain to Muslim individuals. The radical sees the
establishment of the caliphate as a matter of submission to

Allah. The Quran says that the caliphate is promised to the believers (Muslims):

> Allah has promised, to those among you who believe and work righteous deeds, that He will, of a surety, grant them in the land, inheritance (of power), as He granted it to those before them...
> —SURAH 24:55, ALI TRANSLATION

The verse goes on to describe the characteristics of the caliphate—that it will make it easy for Muslims to practice their religion and will give them security in place of fear.

> He will grant them the authority to practise their religion which He has chosen for them (i.e. Islam). And He will surely give them in exchange a safe security after their fear (provided) they (believers) worship Me.

Islam is a religion and a state. After Muhammad emigrated from Mecca to Medina, he set up a political government, established laws, and established Islam as a system of belief that covers every aspect of life.

STRATEGY TO ESTABLISH GLOBAL ISLAMIC AUTHORITY

The radical plans to restore the caliphate by accomplishing three goals:

1. Establish Islamic states.

2. Join these states together under the caliphate.

3. Use the caliphate to submit the entire world to Islamic authority.

To a committed radical who is fighting for his faith, the caliphate means everything and nationality means nothing. His nationality is now belief in Islam.

PILLAR 4: JIHAD IS THE ONLY WAY TO WIN

The Islamic radical is a fundamentalist—he wants to practice Islam the way Muhammad practiced Islam. So his definition of jihad is based on Muhammad's—both in word and by example.

The Quran contains a tremendous amount of teaching about jihad. In fact, I estimate that 60 percent of the Quran is related to the concept of jihad.

Radicals believe non-Muslims who oppress them cause all their problems. Therefore, they readily identify with verses such as these:

> And what is wrong with you that you fight not in the Cause of Allah, and for those weak, ill-treated and oppressed among men, women, and children, whose cry is: "Our Lord! Rescue us from this town whose people are oppressors; and raise for us from You one who will protect, and raise for us from You one who will help."
>
> —SURAH 4:75

> March forth, whether you are light (being healthy, young and wealthy) or heavy (being ill, old and poor), strive hard with your wealth and your lives in the Cause of Allah. This is better for you, if you but knew.
>
> —SURAH 9:41

O you who believe! What (excuse) have you that when it is said to you: Go forth in Allah's way, you should incline heavily to earth; are you contented with this world's life instead of the hereafter? But the provision of this world's life compared with the hereafter is but little. If you do not go forth, He will chastise you with a painful chastisement and bring in your place a people other than you, and you will do Him no harm; and Allah has power over all things.

—SURAH 9:38–39, SHAKIR TRANSLATION

This verse was revealed while Muhammad was preparing his people to go fight in the Campaign of Tabuk. Some Muslims hesitated to go and fight, so this verse warned them that Allah would punish the ones who refused to go and replace them with better people.

In battle, smite the necks

The world was horrified by videotapes of beheadings in Iraq. People wondered why religious radicals would commit this grisly act. The answer is in the Quran:

Therefore, when you meet the Unbelievers (in fight), smite at their necks; at length, when you have thoroughly subdued them, bind a bond firmly (on them)...

—SURAH 47:4, ALI TRANSLATION

PILLAR 5: FAITH IS THE REASON

You will never understand the mind of the Muslim terrorist unless you accept that their foremost motivation is faith. In secular Western society a discussion of a person's faith is practically considered inappropriate and, in certain circumstances, illegal. But it is ridiculous to try to understand a Muslim radical unless you fully accept that he is acting on the basis of faith.

I run the risk of being accused of oversimplifying the motives of radicals as exclusively based on faith. So I will acknowledge that circumstances in addition to faith can push a person toward radicalism. In other words, if a person is unemployed and suffering under a corrupt government that claims to be Islamic, radicalism will look like the solution to his problems. But these external motives alone will not grip his heart to the point that he would strap on a bomb and blow himself up in the name of the cause. It is the faith factor.

As radical groups are subdued or broken up, it is the faith factor that germinates new groups all across the Islamic world. To help you understand their rationale, here are the primary principles that underlie their actions.

IF YOU BELIEVE IN ALLAH, YOU WILL OBEY

The Quran says, "Therefore fear not men, but fear Me" (Surah 5:44, ALI TRANSLATION). If you believe in Allah, then you are obligated to follow the command of jihad, the radicals say, even if it means jail, loss of your job, or worse. If you don't follow the commands of Allah, then you don't believe in Allah.

IF YOU BELIEVE IN FATE, YOU WILL OBEY

One of the most important Islamic teachings is about fate. Islam teaches that Allah controls a person's fate—whether a person experiences good or evil and the hour of death. No amount of human effort can change fate. The Quran says, "No person can ever die except by Allah's Leave and at an appointed term" (Surah 3:145). Therefore, say the radicals, death is nothing to fear because it is under Allah's control.

IF YOU BELIEVE IN JUDGMENT, YOU WILL OBEY

Radicals use a Muslim's fear of the Last Day, or judgment, as a very effective motivation for jihad. According to Islamic theology, judgment is followed by "eternal fire or eternal bliss." If a Muslim believes hell is as bad Allah says it is, radicals argue, then the Muslim will do anything the Quran commands in order to avoid going to hell.

IF YOU ARE MARTYRED, YOU WILL WIN PARADISE

Martyrdom is reassurance; the ultimate sacrifice receives the ultimate reward. Islam teaches that on Judgment Day a man's deeds are weighed, and then Allah decides if he may enter Paradise. If you live as an infidel, you may be sure of going to hell, but if you live the best Muslim life you possibly can, you still have no guarantee of entering Paradise, as the quote from the Quran explained. There is only one guarantee—martyrdom.

The Prophet Muhammad stated, "The person who participates in (Holy battles) in Allah's cause and nothing compels him to do so except belief in Allah and His Apostles, will be recompensed by Allah either with a reward, or booty (if he survives) or will be admitted to Paradise (if he is killed in the battle as a martyr)."[1]

To the radical, death as a martyr is not defeat; it is the gateway to Paradise.

YOU AND YOUR FAITH ARE SUPERIOR TO OTHERS

A repeated theme in radical teaching is that the believer is superior to secular society—superior in faith, in understanding and concept of the nature of the world, in values and standards, in conscience and understanding, and in law and life. Radicals believe that society persecutes them because of their faith. Therefore, when a Western country takes military action against an Islamic country, many Muslims interpret it as an attack against Allah and Islamic faith.

CONCLUSION

From all the information in the chapter we can clearly see what kind of faith it is that causes radical Muslims to go to extremes. It is the call for a restoration of morality and defense of Islam combined with fear of hell and the belief that martyrdom is the only way to ensure access to Paradise.

The next section of this book takes you to the source where the terrorists found their Five Pillars of Radical Philosophy—the lives of Muhammad and his followers.

SECTION II

THE ROOTS
OF TERRORISM
IN ISLAM

Chapter 3

CORE BELIEFS OF ISLAM

The Mind-Set of Violence

WHEN I WAS a freshman at Al-Azhar University in 1980, I enrolled in class called Quranic Interpretation. Two times a month we would gather to hear lectures from a blind sheikh whose passion for Islam made him popular among the students.

Yet his radical side was obvious. Anytime he encountered a reference in the Quran to Christians or Jews, he took great delight in referring to the Christians as "infidels" and Jews as "the children of pigs." He made it clear that he wanted to bring back the glory days of the Islamic empire through jihad.

One day he gave us students an opportunity to ask questions. I stood up and asked him something I had been wondering about for a long time: "Why is it that you teach us all the time about jihad? What about the other verses in the Quran that talk about kindness and forgiveness?"

Immediately his face turned red. I could see his anger, but I could also see that he chose to control it. Instead of yelling at me, he took the chance to reinforce his position in front of the five hundred students who were listening. "My brother," he said, "there is a whole surah [chapter] called 'Spoils of War.' There is no surah called 'Peace.' Jihad and killing are the head of Islam. If you take them out, you cut off the head of Islam."

Today that man is locked up in a prison in the United

States. His name is Omar Abdel Rahman, and he was convicted of masterminding the first bomb attack of the World Trade Center, which occurred in 1993.

Before he came to America, he was the spiritual leader of the radical Egyptian group al-Jihad, which carried out the assassination of Egyptian president Anwar al-Sadat. Later in this book I will tell the incredible story of how Sheikh Abdel Rahman talked the Egyptian Supreme Court into setting him free, which gave him the ability to travel to the United States and practice jihad there.

ISLAM 202

As you can see from this story and from my testimony, I have lived close to terrorism for most of my lifetime. People in the West have a hard time understanding terrorists. They wonder, "Are they just all crazy?"

I can assure you, these people are not lunatics. Nor are they psychopaths who find psychological pleasure in hurting others. No, they are following a philosophy, and once you understand this philosophy, none of their actions will even surprise you.

In this chapter I will tell you the basics of Islam, but we are going to move beyond that very quickly in order to explain the specific religious doctrine that motivates an Islamic terrorist. I will also explain how fundamentalists do away with the verses in the Quran that speak of living in peace and harmony.

SUBMITTING TO ALLAH

The word *Islam* means "submission"; the word *Muslim* means "one who submits to Allah." The Quran says you cannot be a true Muslim unless you submit.

O you who believe! Obey Allah and obey the
Messenger (Muhammad) and those of you (Muslims)
who are in authority.

—SURAH 4:59, THE NOBLE QURAN

Now the question you must answer when submitting
to Allah is, what are Allah's requirements? The answers
are found in the holy books of Islam—the Quran and the
hadith. These teachings also serve as the foundation of
Sharia, or Islamic law.

THE QURAN

The Quran was started in AD 610 when Muhammad, the
prophet of Islam, said the angel Gabriel spoke to him while
he was meditating in a cave near Mecca. Muhammad
stated these were the words of the one true god—Allah.
Muhammad's twelve companions wrote down these words
from Allah as Muhammad received them over a period of
about twenty-two years. In short the Quran is considered
to be Allah's words. It is significant that the revelations
did not all come at the same time, as we will see later.

BOOKS OF HADITH

The books of hadith are another set of holy writings. These
books contain the reports of what Muhammad said and
did during his life. In other words, the books of hadith
give the teachings of Muhammad in word and example.
As Muhammad is considered the perfect example for any
committed Muslim, the hadiths, also known as the record
of the *Sunnah,* have about the same authority for Muslims
as the Quran.

Here's how the books of hadith were created. People
who were close to Muhammad, such as his friends or

wives, observed and recorded his activities. Scholars collected these writings, verified their authenticity and put those hadith that they accepted as true and reliable into six sets of books known as the correct books *(sahih)* of hadith. These books are referenced by the name of the person who originally collected the stories together, for example, hadith by Sahih Al-Bukhari.

The majority of the Muslim world considers these six books of hadith to be authoritative. (To be specific, Sunni Muslims accept all six books. Shiite Muslims accept most hadith, but reject the hadith recorded by the second wife of Muhammad.)

SHARIA (ISLAMIC LAW)

The contents of the Quran and hadith are the basis of *Sharia*, or Islamic law, which describes the duty of Muslims toward the God of Islam.

There are several Sunni and Shiite schools of thought, but all are in agreement that the highest authority for law under Islam is the Quran. So any judgment expressed in the Quran must be accepted and cannot be abrogated by any other source. For areas not addressed in the Quran, the legal scholars turn to the example of Muhammad for guidance. For areas not addressed by Muhammad's life, the legal scholars look to the life of Muhammad's companions. For areas not addressed by the companions, the scholars apply several methods of interpretation to develop new rulings. This process is known as *ishtihad*. The legal opinions developed by Islamic jurists *(fatwas)* become part of Islamic law.

Qutb al-Fiqh is the word used for the books that describe Islamic law. These are not specific books, such as the books of hadith. These books are a whole body of literature, some ancient and some modern.

REQUIREMENTS TO BE A MUSLIM

So what does the Quran and hadith say that Allah wants people to do? There are five key requirements that must be met in order to be a Muslim. These requirements are known as the five pillars of Islam:

1. *Statement of belief.* There must be acceptance of the Muslim statement of faith: "There is no god but Allah, and Muhammad is his prophet."

2. *Prayer.* Muslims are to pray five times a day while facing Mecca, the birthplace of Muhammad. Prayers are at dawn, afternoon, late afternoon, after sunset and night. Special prayers are on Fridays.

3. *Giving alms.* This is similar to a tax. It is paid at the end of the year and distributed to those in need.

4. *Fasting.* This takes place during the Islamic month of Ramadan, which starts at the first visual sighting of the ninth crescent moon according to the Islamic calendar. During this fast Muslims do not eat or drink during daylight hours. A light meal and a large amount of water are taken in before daybreak. After the sun sets, a heavier meal is eaten, and a large amount of liquid is consumed.

5. *Pilgrimage.* Muslims are encouraged to
make a pilgrimage at least once in their lifetimes to Mecca where a five-day ritual is
followed.[1]

Why is it so important that Muslims do what Allah
requires? It's because Islam is a religion of works. Entrance
to Paradise (heaven) must be earned. The sad part is that
Muslims can never have assurance of salvation. When
they die, they believe that they go to the grave, where they
await their judgment at resurrection day.

When judgment day comes, Allah weighs the good
works and the bad works and decides their fate.

Then as for him whose balance (of good deeds) will
be heavy, he will live a pleasant life (in Paradise). But
as for him whose balance (of good deeds) will be light,
he will have his home in *Hawiyah* (pit, i.e., Hell).
—SURAH 101:6–9, THE NOBLE QURAN

Even if you do good works all your life, you have no
guarantee of Paradise. It all depends on what Allah decides.

GUARANTEED ENTRANCE TO PARADISE

There is only one way to guarantee entrance into Paradise—
and this makes the perfect motive for suicide bombers and
jihad fighters. The only way to know for sure that you will
get into Paradise is to die in jihad—to die while striving
for the cause of Allah and fighting the enemy of Islam.

Jihad simply means striving for the cause of Allah,
and it is commonly understood by radicals as meaning
Muslims must fight the enemy of Allah until the enemies
die or the Muslims die. The word *jihad* actually means

"struggle." Jihad has even been defined in legal terms by Islamic *fiqh* as follows:

> [Jihad] is fighting anybody who stands in the way of spreading Islam. Or fighting anyone who refuses to enter into Islam (based on Surah 8:39).

If you die in jihad, you don't even have to go to the grave and wait for judgment; you go directly to Paradise.

Jihad is really a contract between Allah and the Muslim. If the Muslim fights, Allah rewards him in the afterlife.

> Let those (believers) who sell the life of this world for the Hereafter fight in the Cause of Allah, and whoso fights in the Cause of Allah, and is killed or gets victory, We shall bestow on him a great reward.
> —SURAH 4:74, THE NOBLE QURAN

In reference to those who fight jihad, the Quran also says:

> For them Allah has got ready Gardens (Paradise) under which rivers flow, to dwell therein forever. That is the supreme success.
> —SURAH 9:89, THE NOBLE QURAN

When a person dies in jihad, a different burial procedure is followed. After a regular person dies, his body is washed and dressed nicely, as if going to the mosque. When a person dies in jihad, his body is not washed or given clean clothes. That person goes into the coffin just as he died. The blood is a witness for him in front of Allah—a sign of honor. Muslims believe the angels will treat him as a special person to Allah.

Western media have poked fun at the Muslim understanding of Paradise (heaven)—virgins for men to enjoy and so forth—but it is much more significant to recognize that dying in jihad is the only way a Muslim can be assured of entering Paradise at all. This is why you see Muslims leaving their own nations to fight jihad in other countries. Their motivation is religious, which is much more dangerous than a political motivation.

Jihad is definitely commanded for all Muslims in the Quran, but right now let's answer an important question many people ask: "What about all the 'nice' verses in the Quran?"

"But What About..."

You have probably heard on television or read in the print media about verses in the Quran that speak positively about Christians or verses that encourage kindness and promote even religious freedom. You may have wondered, "Are those verses really there?"

Here is the solution to the mystery: the Quran is filled with contradictions. You can find verses where Christians are complimented as well as verses where Christians are condemned to hell.

There are contradictions about other subjects as well. For example, there was much drinking of alcohol in Arabian society during Muhammad's day. One revelation told Arabs to stop drinking alcohol when going to mosque for prayer, but when prayers were finished they could resume drinking. Later another verse came and prohibited alcohol all the time. (Compare Surah 2:219 and Surah 5:90.)

Another example is the relationship between Muslims and Christians. Some verses say that Muslims can have a good relationship with them, but other verses say Muslims are required to convert them to Islam.

In the beginning of Islam the women were not forced to wear a *hijab*, but in subsequent verses, women were commanded to stay in the house and wear a cover.

Islamic scholars had to determine, therefore, which verses to follow in the case of a contradiction. This was accomplished by the principle of abrogation *(naskh).*

The principle of abrogation is based on the fact that the Quran was revealed to Muhammad at different times over a period of about twenty-two years. Some parts of the Quran came earlier, others came later. To solve a contradiction, they decided that new revelations would override or abrogate previous revelations.

There are at least 114 verses in the Quran that speak of kindness and forgiveness, especially in the surah titled "The Heifer" (Surah 2:62, 109). But when Surah 9:5 was revealed later, it canceled out those previous verses. This verse states:

> Fight and slay the Pagans wherever you find them, and seize them, beleaguer them, and lie in wait for them in every strategem (of war); but if they repent, and establish regular prayers and practise regular charity, then open the way for them: for Allah is Oft-forgiving, Most Merciful.
> —ALI TRANSLATION

This is known as the verse of the sword, and it explains that Muslims must fight anyone who chooses not to convert to Islam, whether they are inside or outside of Arabia. It is considered to represent the final development of jihad in Islam.[2]

The principle of abrogation is very strong. If a verse is abrogated, it is as if the earlier verse had not even existed.

You might ask, "Why are there contradictions in the

Quran in the first place? Why did the revelations change over time?" That question can be answered by looking at the life of Muhammad, the prophet of Islam.

At first the messages that were revealed to Muhammad were peaceful and kind in order to attract people. But circumstances changed.

Muhammad encountered much opposition in Mecca, the city where he first preached his message, so he left in AD 622. He went to Yathrib, the city now known as Medina, and built up military strength and a larger number of followers. (Both Mecca and Medina are located in present-day Saudi Arabia.) Later when Muhammad had reached a position of power, he was able to return and conquer Mecca and surrounding areas. This move marks the major change of Islam from a spiritual religion to a political revolution.

The prophet Muhammad's early life in Mecca was all about prayers and meditation, so the Quranic revelations of the Meccan time talk about peace and cooperation with others. But in Medina Muhammad became a military leader and invader, so the revelations in Medina talk about military power and invasion in the name of Islam (jihad).

Sixty percent of the Quranic verses talk about jihad, which stands to reason because Muhammad received most of the Quran after he left Mecca. Jihad became the basic power and driving force of Islam.

It would be nice if the surahs in the Quran were organized in the order that they were revealed, but they are not. Some versions of the Quran will identify each verse as to whether it was revealed in Mecca or Medina; however, you must go to more scholarly references to know the exact order of the revelations.

SUMMARY

In this chapter you have learned some very necessary concepts that will help you to understand the mind-set of an Islamic terrorist. In summary this is what they believe:

- Islam requires submission to Allah, whose words are written in the Quran.

- On Judgment Day Allah weighs your good and bad works and decides whether you go to Paradise or hell.

- Allah stated in the Quran that if you die in jihad, then you are spared judgment and automatically go to Paradise.

- The verses in the Quran that speak of jihad abrogate (cancel out) the verses that speak of love and kindness.

- Jihad is the motivation behind almost every act of terrorism that is done in the name of Islam.

The Quran gives a great deal of practical teaching on the subject of jihad because it was so much a part of Muhammad's life in Medina. The next chapter will give Quranic verses about practicing jihad and address the question of whether all Muslims believe this.

Chapter 4

HOLY WAR IN THE QURAN

Fighting Unbelievers Until They Are Subdued

W E FIND JIHAD as a command to all Muslims enforced by the Quran. The focus of jihad is to overcome people who do not accept Islam. In Muhammad's time jihad was therefore practiced on a regular basis against Christians and Jews, as well as against idol worshippers and anyone who did not convert to Islam. (See Surah 2:217; 4:71–104; 8:24–36, 39–65.) Let's let the Quran speak for itself.

> Those who reject Islam must be killed. If they turn back (from Islam), take (hold of) them and kill them wherever you find them...
> —SURAH 4:89, THE NOBLE QURAN

> So, when you meet (in fight—*Jihad* in Allah's Cause) those who disbelieve, smite (their) necks till when you have killed and wounded many of them, then bind a bond firmly (on them, i.e. take them as captives).
> —SURAH 47:4, THE NOBLE QURAN

> O you who believe! Fight those of the disbelievers who are close to you, and let them find harshness in you; and know that Allah is with those who are *Al-Muttaqun* (the pious).
> —SURAH 9:123, THE NOBLE QURAN

Allah commanded the prophet Muhammad to enforce killing rather than taking prisoners.

> It is not for a Prophet that he should have prisoners of war (and free them with ransom) until he had made a great slaughter (among his enemies) in the land.
>
> —SURAH 8:67, THE NOBLE QURAN

Muslims were told to prepare themselves to fight against the unbelievers.

> Let not the Unbelievers think that they can get the better (of the godly): they will never frustrate them. Against them make ready your strength to the utmost of your power, including steeds of war, to strike terror into (the hearts of) the enemies, of Allah and your enemies, and others besides, whom you may not know, but whom Allah knows.
>
> —SURAH 8:59–60, ALI TRANSLATION

JEWS AND CHRISTIANS ARE ENEMIES OF ISLAM

In the Quran Christians and Jews are called the "People of the Book" in reference to the Scriptures that they follow. At first the Quranic revelations encouraged Muslims to live at peace with Christians. But after Muhammad's move to Medina, the revelations regarding all "People of the Book" became very hostile.

The following verse is considered to be the final revelation from Allah regarding Christians and Jews; therefore, it is understood to override all other revelations. It states:

> And fight them until there is no more *Fitnah* (disbelief and polytheism, i.e., worshipping others besides

Allah) and the religion (worship) will all be for
Allah Alone [in the whole of the world]. But if they
cease (worshipping others besides Allah), then certainly, Allah is All-Seer of what they do.
—SURAH 8:39, THE NOBLE QURAN

In other words, this verse says, "Fight those who reject
Islam until all the worship is for Allah alone." The Quran
also says Muslims must not be friends with Christians or
Jews.

Take not the Jews and the Christians as *Auliya*
(friends, protectors, helpers), they are but *Auliya* of
each other. And if any amongst you takes them (as
Auliya), then surely he is one of them.
—SURAH 5:51

This fact is also emphasized in Surah 5:52–57 and Surah
4:89. When fighting Christians, the Quran tells Muslims to
punish them severely so they will be dispersed (Surah 8:57).

The Quran commands Muslims to force Christians and
Jews to convert to Islam with very strong and direct words.
The following is from *The Noble Quran* in English, which
includes commentary in the parentheses.

O you who have been given the Scripture (Jews and
Christians)! Believe in what We have revealed (to
Muhammad) confirming what is (already) with you,
before We efface faces (by making them like the
back of necks; without nose, mouth, eyes) and turn
them hindwards, or curse them as We cursed the
Sabbath-breakers. And the commandment of Allah
is always executed.
—SURAH 4:47

Just in case the meaning is not crystal clear, this translation has a footnote at the bottom of the page that reads, "This Verse is a severe warning to the Jews and Christians, and an absolute obligation that they must believe in Allah's Messenger Muhammad and in his Message of Islamic Monotheism and in this Quran."

CONVINCING THE MUSLIMS TO GO FIGHT

When you read these Quranic verses, it is helpful to think of them in their historical context. Allah told Muhammad to go out and conquer the world, so many Quranic verses were given that encouraged the people to fight jihad. Here are some examples:

> Allah has preferred in grades those who strive hard and fight with their wealth and their lives above those who sit (at home). Unto each, Allah has promised good (Paradise), but Allah has preferred those who strive hard and fight above those who sit (at home) by a huge reward.
> —SURAH 4:95, THE NOBLE QURAN

Those who did not participate in jihad were threatened with hell fire.

> ...they hated to strive and fight, with their goods and their persons, in the cause of Allah: they said, "Do not go forth in the heat." Say, "The fire of Hell is fiercer in heat." If only they could understand!
> —SURAH 9:81, ALI TRANSLATION

Those who retreat would incur Allah's wrath.

If any do turn his back to them on such a day—
unless it be in a stratagem of war, or to retreat to a
troop (of his own)—he draws on himself the wrath
of Allah, and his abode is Hell—an evil refuge
(indeed)!

—SURAH 8:16, ALI TRANSLATION

Obviously you can see that killing, or jihad, is not an
option. It is a must because it is Allah's command (Surah
9:29). Every Muslim is required to participate to fulfill
his faith. The only exceptions are those who are disabled,
blind, and crippled (Surah 4:95)

ISLAM'S ULTIMATE GOAL

Jihad is carried out in order to achieve the ultimate goal of
Islam—to establish Islamic authority over the whole world.
Islam is not just a religion; it is a government too. That
is why it always gets down to politics. Islam teaches that
Allah is the only authority; therefore, political systems
must be based on Allah's teaching and nothing else.

The Quran states:

If any do fail to judge by (the light of) what Allah has
revealed, they are (no better than) Unbelievers....If
they fail to judge by (the light of) what Allah has
revealed, they are (no better than) those who rebel.

—SURAH 5:44, 47, ALI TRANSLATION

People fighting jihad consider themselves to have succeeded when a nation declares Islam as both their religion and their form of government. Nations where this
has been accomplished include Afghanistan (under the
Taliban), Iran (through Ayatollah Khomeini's revolution),
and Sudan (under Hasan al-Turabi). The Islamic radical

army known as ISIS gained control of geographic areas in 2015, but not entire countries.

Man-made political systems—from democracies to dictatorships—are considered invalid. Moderate Muslims, however, do not always agree with this. A good example is past Egyptian president Anwar al-Sadat. He pronounced that there would be "no politics in Islam and no Islam in politics."

This statement was unacceptable to my former university professor Sheikh Omar Abdel Rahman, who had become the spiritual leader of the Egyptian terrorist organization al-Jihad. After President Sadat said those words, Sheikh Abdel Rahman declared that the president was an infidel apostate who should be killed. Following Islamic law, al-Jihad carried out the declaration of its leader and shot the president to death. President Sadat paid the ultimate price—his life—in an effort to stop Islam from becoming the governing authority in Egypt in the 1980s.

In the 1980s radical Islamic groups focused their attacks on their own governments. Now these organizations are turning to attack the West directly. Later in this book I will explain why.

Now You Know the Basics

Now you know the key facts of Islam. In contrast, let's look at what the media have been telling us.

Chapter 5

MISINFORMED BY THE MEDIA

Making Islam Look Good to the West

O NE OF THE indirect results of the events of September 11, 2001, was a wave of attention in the media regarding Islam. Islam was almost always represented as a religion of peace. It was made to be palatable to the Western ears.

The experts who were interviewed tried to separate the religious side of Islam from its political side, which cannot be done. When you see a Muslim on TV or print media saying that Islam is a religion of peace, it can be explained one of two ways:

1. *Wishful thinking.* Although this is not the Islam taught in the Quran, this person really wishes that it were. He sincerely believes he can explain away the unpalatable parts.

2. *Deceit with the intent to attract converts.* This is jihad practiced a different way. Instead of killing the enemy, you convert them with lies.

WISHFUL THINKING

An excellent example of wishful thinking about Islam is the show aired by popular talk-show host Oprah Winfrey. "Islam 101" aired on October 5, 2001—after the attack against America but before the United States took action in Afghanistan.

Oprah had a few Muslim guests on the show to educate the audience about the basics of Islam. One of the show's guests that day was thirty-one-year-old Queen Rania, the modern, Westernized queen of Jordan. Oprah asked her to comment on whether women in Islam were equal to men.

First of all, asking Queen Rania about anything in Islam is like asking Michael Jackson about his Christianity and what the Bible really teaches. Nevertheless the queen and the other Muslim women on the show acted as if they were the highest authorities on Islam. With great conviction, the queen stated, "Islam views women as full and equal partners to men, so [women's] rights are guaranteed by Islam."[1]

Her answers made Western viewers feel good, but they do not accurately reflect the teachings of the Quran regarding women. If women are equal to men, why does the Quran say:

1. A Muslim man can be married to four women at the same time, but a Muslim woman can only be married to one man. "Marry (other) women of your choice, two or three, or four" (Surah 4:3, *The Noble Quran*).

2. Men have the right to ask for a divorce, but not women (Surah 2:229).

3. Women only inherit half of what men inherit (Surah 4:11).

4. Women may not serve as imams, and they are not allowed to lead prayer in the

presence of men. (Man must always be above woman according to Surah 4:34.)

5. A woman is not allowed to answer the door at home if her husband is not there, even if it's her brother or a relative at the door. (This is derived from Surah 33:53, where Muhammad was giving instructions to people who visited his home. He said that if he wasn't home, they had to speak to his wives through a screen.)

6. Women should stay in their houses (Surah 33:33). Many Muslim women cannot travel without the permission of their fathers or husbands.

7. If a wife refuses to have sexual relations with her husband, it is permissible for the husband to physically beat her until she submits (Surah 4:34).

8. During Jihad, when a man dies, he goes to heaven and Allah rewards him with incredible energy to enjoy sex with seventy virgins the first night. What happens if a woman dies in jihad? What is her reward—to be one of the seventy?

I am not sure whom the queen was trying to convince—herself or the world. The prophet Muhammad once said, "If there is an evil omen in anything, it is in the house, the woman, and the horse."[2]

Oprah also questioned Queen Rania about the veil (*hijab*) that some Muslim women wear. The queen said,

"It's a personal choice. Some people are more conservative than others." She pointed out that she herself chooses not to wear one.[3]

About the issue of the veil in Islam, the following are the Quranic verses that command women to cover themselves.

> O Prophet! Tell your wives and your daughters and the women of the believers to draw their cloaks (veils) all over their bodies (i.e. screen themselves completely except the eyes or one eye to see that way).
> —SURAH 33:59, THE NOBLE QURAN

> And stay in your houses, and do not display yourselves like that of the times of ignorance…
> —SURAH 33:33, THE NOBLE QURAN

The only people allowed to see a woman's face are her husband, children, siblings, and parents:

> It is no sin on them (the Prophet's wives, if they appear unveiled) before their fathers, or their sons, or their brothers, or their brother's sons, or the sons of their sisters, or their own (believing) women, or their (female) slaves.
> —SURAH 33:55, THE NOBLE QURAN

Islamic law has generalized these instructions to Muhammad's wives to apply to all women. (See Surah 24:31.) Queen Rania and other wishful thinkers like her do not recognize that they cannot interpret the Quran to suit their own preferences.

Oprah Winfrey's show was just another opportunity for these Muslim women to present the secular, Westernized, compromised, and Christianized Islam that is not supported by the Quran and Islamic teaching. I hope that

Oprah will find out the truth about Islam and present the correct information on this subject.

DECEIT

During one of my visits to the United States in August of 1998, I was staying with a family friend near Los Angeles. As we were surfing through TV channels, an Islamic program caught our attention. To my amazement I heard the announcer say, "In a minute we will enjoy a spiritual journey through the prophet Muhammad's life with Brother Paul."

I did not move from the television set until I saw Brother Paul. I almost hit the floor when I laid eyes on him. He was a dark man with black hair and a thick, long, black beard, and he was wearing a long white robe and a tiny little head covering. Paul probably graduated from some Islamic institute in the Middle East and came to the United States as a missionary to spread Islam in the West.

I'm thinking, "Paul? Paul is a Muslim name now? This guy is 100 percent Middle East Muslim who grew up just like me. There is no way that is his real name." What flabbergasted me was how Brother Paul used familiar Christian lingo such as, "The Lord bless you; the grace of our Lord be with you; God bless you." He talked about God the Creator and how mankind can have a relationship with Him, how we can hear His voice and He can hear our prayers, and that we should allow the Spirit of God to work in us.

My head was spinning listening to this program that was broadcast from California. I was thinking, "Now I understand how they are spreading Islam in the US and Europe." I jumped out of my seat and cried out, "O God, have mercy on America! God, protect America and Your people in this great country. Please expose this great deception! Rescue this nation from this great deception!"

My friend and his family tried to comfort me by saying, "God's protective hand has been on America since day one, and it will always be."

I asked my friend, "Why is this man lying to Americans about his name? Why would he present to America a new Islam that is totally different from the one that I grew up experiencing for most of my life? Why would he present an Islam that is much closer to Christianity than to the real Islam that I studied for so many years?" I told my friend, "This man should tell America his real name. Most likely it is Muhammad, Ahmed, Mahmoud, Mustaffa, Omar, or Osama—not Paul."

This was the first time I witnessed Muslims presenting a totally new Islam to the West. The average Muslim from the Middle East would never recognize it as the Islam that he practiced.

It is now obvious that many Islamic leaders are doing their part for jihad by influencing the Western media. Yes, they are doing their part when they fool the majority by getting them to believe that Islam is not for killing; that it is only a religion, not a political system; and that it is for peace, love, forgiveness, and so on. That will keep Islam the fastest-growing religion in the world. It is just a different practice of the same principles of jihad.

Remember, Muslims declared jihad worldwide, but every Muslim is using a different strategy. One is using guns and bombs, and another is using words and lies to increase the numbers of Muslims worldwide. The method makes no difference; they are both sincere Muslims, and it is one jihad according to the Quran—jihad against the enemies of Allah who resist the spread of Islam worldwide.

What amazes me is the audacity of these people. They hung the American flag over their centers, schools, mosques, and Islamic institutes. They posted signs saying, "God Bless America" or "United We Stand." In the meantime their fellow Muslims in the Middle East were burning American flags and posting signs supporting bin Laden and his act of terrorism on America.

In all fairness some "wishful thinking" Muslims really did support America at this time. But other Muslims were doing what was simply expedient at the moment. They are a good example of Islamic politics in non-Islamic lands. These Muslims will lie and say things they do not believe at any moment as long as doing so would help Islam. Their loyalty is to Islam, not to the nation where they are living.

NATIONAL LOYALTY

I know that many people will disagree with me by saying, "There are many American and European Muslims who are loyal and sincere to their countries. After all, these countries have been their homes for many years." I would like to address this comment by pointing out that Islam does not believe in the national organization of non-Islamic peoples or any countries that do not follow Islamic law.

In Islamic law there are only two types of nations—a nation that is of the house of Islam or a nation that is of the house of war. We all know that America and most of the European countries are not of "the house of Islam," meaning they do not live by the Islamic law; therefore, they are the "house of war."

Any good Muslim who is living according to Allah's law

and the Quran will never choose loyalty to their citizenship over loyalty to Islam. This is not personal opinion; this is 100 percent Islamic law.

A good example of this is the way Egyptians, Algerians, Sudanese, Saudis, and many others deny their citizenship and loyalty to their countries when they became members of one of the fundamentalist movements. These movements teach their members, "Islam is your flesh and blood."

All of the fundamentalist movements in the Arabic countries prohibit their members from serving in the military or defending their countries. They believe they should not support apostate and infidel countries that do not apply Islamic law to the whole country.

Shokri Moustafa, a person you will learn much more about later in the book, took this principle to an even higher level. His movement prohibited its members from working in any government job.

Muslims who have any sense of loyalty to Islam will have a hard time justifying loyalty to their country if that country is not Islamic. The true Muslim believes that the whole world is his home and that he is commanded to submit the world to the authority of Islam. A sincere believer of Islam will not die for a patch of dirt called the homeland, but he is willing to die for Islam and Islamic holy places.

When you see Palestinians fighting and dying, understand that non-Muslims or shallow Muslim Palestinians are fighting for the land, but true Muslim Palestinians (Hamas) are passionate because they are fighting the enemies of Allah and defending an Islamic holy place, i.e., the Dome of the Rock in Jerusalem.

Muslims believe that the Dome of the Rock is the third most important holy place in Islam.[4] The prophet

Muhammad told his followers that Allah miraculously transported him from the Arabian Desert to this place in Jerusalem and anointed him as imam to lead prayers for all of Allah's missionaries and prophets who came from heaven that day. After the prayer the prophet Muhammad said he went to heaven to meet with Allah. (This is known as the Miraculous Night Journey [*Al-Asrah waal MahRag*].)

Groups of Palestinians are fighting the same enemy for different reasons. One group is fighting for some land that they can call home and establish a government—perhaps a communist government, according to George Habash's leadership. Habash has a Christian name, but he is not Christian; it's just his name. Another group wants the land so it can establish a socialist government according to the mind-set of the former renovation engineer and businessman Yasser Arafat.

The final group is the die-hard Muslim Palestinians who look at the other two groups as betrayers who abuse the name of Palestinians to gain power. This group is the Hamas movement, founded by Sheikh Ahmed Yassin.

TELLING TRUE FROM FALSE

At this point I think you will be able to do a much better job of telling true from false when you see what amounts to Islamic propaganda in the media.

Chapter 6

HUMAN RIGHTS UNDER ISLAM

Balancing Respect With Freedom of Speech and Freedom of Religion

MUSLIM FUNDAMENTALISTS ARE in constant battle with writers, authors, and other media figures who express their opinions openly in the free world. Many people have sacrificed their lives because they had a different opinion than that of Muslim fundamentalists.

For example, on January 7, 2015, radical Muslims attacked the French satirical magazine *Charlie Hebdo* and killed twelve editors of that magazine for their satirical depictions of prophet Muhammad.

I strongly believe that the free world must not practice self-censorship in the face of threats and intimidation from any group in the world, including Muslims. Free people must not limit human rights because of those who want to impose their understanding of Islamic law upon the whole world. Freedom of speech is worthless if it is not exercised. But I believe that we should have enough respect not to hurt religious feelings in a reckless way. What the West views as freedom of speech, the Islamic world perceives as an intentional insult to their beliefs, and usually even the most moderate Muslims will react in an emotional way to this.

I was very sad when I saw the reaction of the French president, the millions of people in France, and the key leaders from all over the world, who joined the demonstrations to support the actions of the magazine. I did not hear any of them apologize for the violation of the religious feelings of Muslims, Jews, and Christians. All you would hear was the defense of the freedom of speech, without even considering the freedom of religion.

When *Charlie Hebdo* continued publishing satirical depictions of Muhammad, the Muslim world was outraged, and as a reaction forty-five churches were set on fire in Niger in a weekend of protests. This kind of reaction from the Muslim world was predictable and could have been prevented.

Please note that the real issue is not about making an image of Muhammad; it is about insulting Muhammad. The Muslim world was not necessarily protesting the image; it was protesting the insult. In fact, I used an artist's drawing of Muhammad on the cover of my book titled *Coffee With the Prophet*. The image was a professional and accurate depiction of what Muhammad looked like according to Muslim sources. This image is not insulting or offensive, and it did not cause any more reaction in the Muslim world than the many other historical drawings of Muhammad that are reproduced in textbooks and on the Internet every day.

MUSLIMS TAKING AWAY FREEDOM OF SPEECH FROM OTHER MUSLIMS

Even Muslims themselves are not safe from being judged and punished for expressing ideas that go against the opinions of radicals. A good example of this is Dr. Naguib Mahfouz, who won the 1988 Nobel Prize in literature. Dr. Mahfouz is an Egyptian Muslim, yet radical Muslims tried to murder him in 1994. He was on his way home from work at a university when several men attacked him, stabbing him with knives. They left him in a puddle of blood on one of Cairo's streets. Dr. Mahfouz was eighty-three years old when this happened; I am glad he survived.[1]

Another victim of one of the Islamic movements was Dr. Farag Foda, a moderate Muslim who cared about the country's political survival. He decided to fight the Islamic movement

(Image Courtesy of Sinai Publishing,Cairo, Egypt)
Dr. Farag Foda, shot to death in 1992 by Islamic fundamentalists for writing books exposing their activity.

through his writing. He warned Egypt, the Arabic countries, and the world about the dangers of fundamentalist Islam. He wrote:

> What kind of time in our history is this? This is the time when if someone asks a question the other party answers him with bullets. Many times I asked myself, What is this that we are going through in our Egyptian history? Are we ever going to snap out of it? Is this the time that if you have an opinion, or something to say, you had better get to know how to use a machine gun first or get your black belt in the martial arts? If they think that this will make us back off or stop, they are terribly mistaken. If they think their actions will scare us, they are wrong! If they think for a second that we will rest our pens from writing or our mouths from voicing opinions, they are expecting the impossible. This is not about courage; it's about logic.[2]

Dr. Foda paid the ultimate price for his opinion. He was shot to death in 1992 by the groups he warned against, but his legacy has been a great inspiration to many Egyptian writers.

THE DIFFERENCE BETWEEN A MUSLIM CONVERT AND A CHRISTIAN CONVERT

During a visit to Washington, DC, in the winter of 2000, I heard that the Islamic Society at Georgetown University was hosting a rally for American students. The speaker at the rally was an ex-Baptist minister from Texas who had converted from Christianity to Islam. I had never heard of anything like this before.

I immediately started thinking, "What in the world could happen to an American Baptist pastor that would cause him to make a decision like that?"

I took a friend, and we went to this seminar. We sat in the middle of the room, which was packed with about three hundred students. A little less than half of the students were devout Muslims from overseas. The young men had long beards, and the girls wore the *hijab*.

When I laid my eyes on this man as he entered the room, I couldn't believe what I saw. He was wearing the traditional clothing that Islamic fanatics wear in Egypt. He had the long, white robe and the long, thick beard—all of it. Finally they introduced him as the ex-Christian pastor. They called him Sheikh Yusef.

I listened to this man for almost an hour while he shared a very dry message that showed his tremendous ignorance of Islam and Islamic history. You could almost see it in his face that he was completely lost. He tried hard to convince a young, eager crowd that Islam is the answer to our world's problems today. He delivered an absolutely foreign picture, far from the truth of Islam, the same picture that the Islamic group deceived him with, the same picture that the Islamic organizations use to bait Westerners.

After he finished his talk, he gave an opportunity for comments and questions. Mine was the first hand up. After he gave me permission to speak, I started asking him questions.

"How long has it been since you converted to Islam?"

He replied, "Eight years."

"Good," I said. "Have you faced any type of persecution here in the US since you made this decision?"

"Not at all," he said.

"Did your church or other churches commit their members to go after you and never stop until they killed you because you betrayed Christianity?"

"None of that happened," he said.

"Are there any verses in the Bible that say Christian apostates should be killed?"

"No, there are no verses in the Bible that talk about that."

Now you could see the interest building among the students, but you could see the fear on the face of this ex-pastor. At that moment I introduced myself by saying, "I am a former professor of Al-Azhar University. I taught Islamic history and culture. Eight years ago I left Islam and became a Christian. Do you know what consequences I suffered for leaving Islam? I lost my job at the university. I was put in prison by the secret police who tortured me almost to death. Even my own family pursued me and tried to kill me and several times I suffered attempts of assassination.

"Now it has been eight years exactly, just like you, but the difference between you and me is that I lost everything

I ever had or lived for. I lost my family, job, home country, and right to live. Now I am constantly on the run. The sword of Islam is on my neck all the time because the Quran and the prophet Muhammad made it this way.

"My question for you, pastor, is, what was the price you paid for leaving Christianity? When you made that decision, did anyone start persecuting you? No one tried to kill you or put you in prison. The FBI did not arrest you as if you had committed a terrible crime against your country and your people. No church sentenced you to death or sent out someone to kill you with a sword.

"You, Sheikh Yusef, are still living in your country, secure and protected by great laws. You're free to travel from state to state to share about what you believe, but I can no longer walk along the Nile or set a foot on the soil of my country.

"You grew up free in a free country to make any decision you like until you made this one, to become a Muslim. Sadly, with this decision, you gave up your freedom. I hope you realize that you are no longer free, because the day you think of leaving Islam again, you will be killed by the sword of Islam and will not be able to escape."

Sheikh Yusef had just learned a hard truth about Islam: when you become a slave of Allah, you give up your right to change your religion again.

FREEDOM OF RELIGION

If you have read this far in the book, you don't need me to tell you that freedom of religion is not a part of Islam. In fact, religious persecution is commanded in the Quran. What I can add to that understanding at this point is an example from Holland. In this case Muslim writers condemned a foreign government for offering religious freedom to former Muslims.

The parliament of Holland passed a law that grants political asylum to persons who have left Islam and converted to other religions, such as Christianity. A vehement protest was published in the *Muslim World League Journal*, a magazine published in Mecca, Saudi Arabia. In an article titled "The Right of Political Asylum for Muslim Apostates in Holland" the magazine complained that this decision was made by two Christian political parties in Holland who were "acting as if converting to Christianity is a reason for persecution."[3] What a strange thing to say, since Islamic law states that apostates from Islam must be put to death.

The article claimed that the Christian parties in Holland were trying to entice Muslims to leave their faith in order to secure citizenship in Holland.

> This wicked decision is designed to take advantage of the situation of the Muslims that live in Holland. It is about manipulating the thousands of Muslims struggling to stay legally in Holland. They are pressuring these Muslims to change their religion so that they can get legal status.[4]

The article continued to insult and accuse the church by saying:

> This law is just legalizing the agenda of the Christians and the church which did not succeed in the past to entice the Muslims by all kind of financial and material prizes to get them to change their religion. Now they are using stronger methods [citizenship].[5]

When I read an article like this, my heart goes out to the Muslim world and the tremendous tragedy of human rights in these countries. The most dangerous thing a Muslim can do is leave Islam—no matter what the reason. I personally feel for people who take the courageous step away from Islam. These people live the rest of their lives with the sword of Islam on their necks.

SUMMARY

The chapters in section II of this book have helped you to understand the core beliefs of Islam. In the next section I want to make you an informed person regarding the life of Muhammad. I want you to know how this man lived and the example that he set for Muslims to follow.

SECTION III

FOLLOWING MUHAMMAD'S EXAMPLE

Chapter 7

ARABIAN CULTURE

Taking Advantage of a Violent Mind-Set

WHEN YOU ARE studying a historical figure, it is important to understand the setting and culture in which he lived. For example, Jesus lived in a Jewish community that was under the control of the Romans. His actions and teachings were influenced by the circumstances of His day; for example, He had a teaching regarding paying taxes to Rome: "Give back to Caesar what is Caesar's and to God what is God's" (Mark 12:17).

So to understand Muhammad and Islam, we need to look at the culture of the place where Islam was born. We will discover the roots of terrorism all the way back in seventh-century Arabia. (Arabia is considered to be the peninsula where the modern-day countries of Yemen, Oman, United Arab Emirates, Saudi Arabia, Kuwait, and Jordan are located.) The characteristics of the tribes during this pre-Islam period of history can be described in three major categories.

THE TRIBAL MENTALITY

Before Islam, southwest Asia, also known as the Arabian Desert, was not developed to the point of having any distinct nations or countries. The people were not under the authority of any type of law or government. The only authority was the tribe leader over his members. These tribes were well known for their loyalty to their own tribe cultures. In modern Islamic history what outsiders consider to be unusual loyalty is actually deeply rooted in the Arabic culture before Islam.

EXTREMIST

One of the stronger characteristics of Arabs in Muhammad's time was that they were known for being extremist in everything—extreme love, extreme hate, and no tolerance of others who were different from them. They were not likely to accept any diversity or anyone else's beliefs. Their way was the only way.

During this time of history and culture many Arabs excelled at poetry. One of the older poets described this characteristic of extremism and said, "We are people of no medium, and tolerance is not our way. We get our way, or we will die that day trying." They took a great pride in being extreme and wrote poems about it.

This extremist mentality did not change at all after Islam. As a matter of fact, Islam embraced many of the core characteristics of this Arabic culture. There was no moderation and no reconciliation with others. If two people had a fight, no one would ever walk away. They didn't have the mentality to sit, discuss, and sort out a problem. Their attitude was, "Give me my way or give me death!" As a result, Islamic history is full of bloodshed.

Many non-Arab Muslims, such as Iranians, Afghans, Pakistanis, Indians, and others, have adapted to and adopted these behaviors as the way of their new religion.

CONSTANT POWER STRUGGLE AND FIGHTING

Being courageous and violent was a sign of manhood in seventh-century Arabia. The people of this culture considered being quick to fight as a necessity for survival. Only the strongest survived; therefore, these tribes fought constantly as a way of existence. This mentality was manifested into a basic lifestyle.

- Defend your own tribe and its territory.

- Plunder the possessions of those you defeat. Many individuals and groups would invade others to gain position and wealth.

Islam did not change any of these characteristics or influence the behavior of the Arabs. Instead, Islam embraced the Arab mentality and used it to accomplish its agenda. Jihad (striving for the cause of Allah) as a core belief of Islam came to the Arabic mentality not as a new behavior but as one with which they were very familiar. Islam called on the Arabs to act out their courage and violent ways.

The majority of the Arabs entered Islam so that they would be rewarded with the possessions of people who would not submit to Islam. Islamic history tells us that many times during the early days of Islam, the proper way to divide spoils was an area of controversy among the Arab Muslims.

So we see that Muhammad was born into a culture where conquest and bloodshed were the norm. Now let's see how those norms were incorporated into Islam through the concept of jihad.

Chapter 8

MUHAMMAD DECLARES JIHAD

Jihad Fully Developed in Muhammad's Lifetime

THE IMMIGRATION OF Muhammad from Mecca to Medina was a defining moment in the history of Islam. Everything in the mind-set of the prophet of Islam changed—especially his attitude toward the unbelieving people around him.

In Mecca Muhammad never spoke of jihad. There was no talk of holy war because he did not have military strength, and his movement was small and weak in society. But in Medina, where he built an army, the major topic of Quranic revelation was jihad and fighting the enemy. Revelations increasingly served to motivate Muslims to fight.

Let's compare the differences between Muhammad's life in Mecca and his life in Medina:

- **Mecca:** He invited people to be a part of Islam by preaching.
  Medina: He persuaded people to convert by the sword.

- **Mecca:** He acted as a priest, living a life of prayer, fasting, and worship.
  Medina: He behaved as a military commander, personally leading twenty-seven attacks.

- **Mecca:** He had only one wife, Khadija, for those twelve years.
  Medina: He married twelve more women in ten years.

- **Mecca:** He fought against idol worship.
  Medina: He fought against People of the Book (Jews and Christians).

Muhammad's move from Mecca to Medina changed Islam into a political movement. Dr. Omar Farouk wrote in his book *The Arabs and Islam:*

> The immigration of the prophet of Islam from Mecca to Medina is of great importance in Islamic history. It marks a great revolution in the nature of Islam. Islam went from a religious and spiritual revelation to a political agenda.

I am now going to give you the history of jihad as it was developed and defined in Muhammad's life. Remember, for about twenty-two years Muhammad received Quranic verses from the angel Gabriel. The philosophy of jihad was developed progressively, just as Muhammad's political position was developed progressively. As Muhammad's position in society grew stronger, the revelations about jihad became broader and grander.

MUHAMMAD'S PROBLEMS IN MECCA

One must ask, "Why did Muhammad leave Mecca?" Muhammad spent ten to twelve years in Mecca persuading people to follow Islam without killing them or demanding any taxes from them. His message was one of repentance, patience, and forgiveness. However, there was great tension between him and the tribe he came from. This was the biggest tribe of the area—Quraysh. Many people were abandoning idol worship and following Islam, which the tribal leaders did not like.

At first they tried to make a deal with Muhammad. "We'll make you a king," the tribal leaders told him, "but don't talk about Islam anymore. Or if you want to be wealthy, we'll give you money and make you the wealthiest man in Arabia."

Muhammad happened to be standing next to his uncle when they said this, and he replied, "Oh, my uncle, if they bring the sun and put it in my right hand and bring the moon and put it in my left hand, I will not give up my revelation."

Muhammad negotiated with the leaders from AD 620 to 622, but they never reached an agreement.[1]

The tribe of Quraysh began to persecute him. They threw dirt on his head while he was praying, and they spit on him. They tried to kill him several times. One time they had a lady invite him for a meal and put poison in the lamb she served him. The Quran makes reference to Muhammad's problems at this time:

> And (remember) when the disbelievers plotted against you (O Muhammad) to imprison you, or to kill you, or to get you out (from your home, i.e., Makkah); they were plotting and Allah too was plotting; and Allah is the Best of those who plot.
> —SURAH 8:30, THE NOBLE QURAN

Muhammad did not leave Mecca without thinking, however. He had a plan for what he would do after he left.

FIRST REVELATION OF JIHAD:
REPAY THOSE WHO MISTREAT YOU

Muhammad spent his first year in Medina building up his military strength. The goal of his first jihad, or holy war, was to take revenge on Quraysh, the tribe that had persecuted him. This attitude is no surprise because Muhammad was still influenced by the Arab mentality I described earlier. ("If you cause me one trouble, I will cause you two troubles.")

The Quraysh tribe created wealth through trade. Each year they took one trip to Yemen and one trip to Syria. They took a large caravan of things to sell at their destination, and brought home another load of things to sell at home. They carried a lot of money and valuables.

Muhammad planned to ambush one of the caravans returning to Mecca. He and his army laid wait for them in the Valley of Badr. However, the caravan leader heard about the trap and successfully went home by a different road.

The tribal leaders were very happy the caravan got home, but they were very angry with Muhammad. They decided to teach him a lesson to let everyone in Arabia see that no one played games with the Quraysh tribe. Mecca sent their army to fight Muhammad at Badr. To their shock, Muhammad won a great victory and killed most of the enemy army.

Everyone in Arabia heard about the battle—and they recognized that Muhammad was now the most powerful man in Arabia because he had defeated the most powerful tribe.

THE SECOND REVELATION OF JIHAD:
CONQUER YOUR REGION

After this victory Muhammad said the angel Gabriel brought him a new message: he must fight every tribe in Arabia and make them all submit to Islam. Muhammad declared, "There will not be two religions in Arabia. Arabia will submit only to Islam."[2] As a result, Muhammad no longer focused mainly on converting heathen or idol worshippers. Now the Jews and Christians became targets of persuasion.

This development of jihad came through the following Quranic verse:

> Fight against those who (1) believe not in Allah, (2) nor in the Last Day, (3) nor forbid that which has been forbidden by Allah and His Messenger (Muhammad) (4) and those who acknowledge not the religion of truth (i.e. Islam) among the people of the Scripture (Jews and Christians), until they pay the *Jizyah* [tax] with willing submission, and feel themselves subdued.
> —SURAH 9:29, THE NOBLE QURAN

At first glance this verse is a little hard to understand in English, but it will be very clear after I explain it. This verse says Muslims must fight four kinds of people:

1. Those who don't believe in Allah

2. Those who don't believe in the last day

3. Those who do things that Allah and Muhammad have forbidden

4. Those who don't acknowledge Islam as the truth, i.e., "people of the Scripture," who are the Jews and Christians

Muhammad gave people three options:

1. They could accept the message of Islam.

2. They could remain Jews or Christians but pay a special tax (*jizyah*), which is traditionally levied once a year.

3. They could die. (The phrase "and feel themselves subdued" is much stronger in Arabic than in this English translation. The Arabic word means something like "abject subjection." It carries the idea of someone cowering in fear before a greater power. If abject subjection is not achieved, then death follows.)

The results of Muhammad's options were that the majority accepted the message of Islam, the wealthy unbelievers paid high taxes, and the rest were forced to go to war.

Taxing Christians Today

The tax against Christians is not something that was just practiced in ancient times. Fanatic groups in Egypt still go to Christians and ask for the tax. They will meet with the Christian and explain, "You are Christian. We are Muslim. This is a Muslim country. Our job is to practice the law of Islam. The law says you have two choices—convert to Islam or remain in your faith. It's OK with us if you choose to remain in your faith, but you must pay tax every year to the Islamic authority."

The Egyptian government isn't trying to collect the tax, but these independent groups have taken it upon themselves because the government isn't doing it.

So the Christian is presented with the tax, which is usually a sizeable sum of money based on his income. The Christian may say, "I don't have the money right now.

Give me a few days to pull it together." So the radicals will go away and come back in a few days.

The Christian may again say, "Please, give me another week." So they will go away and come back in a week. But if the Christian still doesn't have the money, there are no more chances. You can be sure they will come back and kill him—probably shoot him to death.

I have a Christian friend from Egypt who is now a university professor in the United States. His two Christian brothers, a medical doctor and a pharmacist, were living in Egypt, and the radicals came and asked for the tax. These Christians refused, and they were both killed.

FINANCING JIHAD

The tax on unbelievers was one way Muhammad raised money, but his most important source of income was plundering after battle. This was his economic lifeblood, just as oil is the economic life of the Gulf countries today. They did not farm, work trades, or conduct business. They fought.

Part of their profit came from slave trading. When invading an enemy country, they killed all males and took the women and children as slaves. During that time the Arabian Desert became famous for slave trading.

Of his plundering, Muhammad said:

> All income that comes by the hooves of horses and the point of the sword is a gift from Allah. Allah provides for those who fight. But if they go back to their old trades, they will just earn a living the normal way.[3]

Muhammad had an agreement with his military regarding the plunder taken from defeated enemies.

Muhammad got to keep 20 percent, and the army could divide the remaining 80 percent among themselves. This sounds pretty good, except his army could have as many as ten thousand men. So each man in the army got .008 percent compared to Muhammad's 20 percent.

Muhammad's army started rebelling and complaining against him because they said they didn't get to keep enough of the plunder. The situation looked as if it would get out of control until Muhammad received a new revelation.

> And know that out of all the booty that you may acquire (in war), a fifth share is assigned to Allah,— and to the Messenger, and to near relatives, orphans, the needy, and the wayfarer...
> —SURAH 8:41, ALI TRANSLATION

This entire surah (chapter) was titled "The Spoils of War." It specifically mentions the Battle of Badr. If you want a good overview of the military mind-set of Muhammad, read this chapter.

The invasion of Uhud

This was the second war that the prophet Muhammad and new converts fought against the Arabs who rejected the call of Islam. After the fight the military leaders and the personal guard of Muhammad faced a major conflict. The disagreement was over plundering the possessions of the enemy. The military leaders told the personal guard of Muhammad that they should take part in the plundering of possessions. "If we didn't fight, there would be no victory," they argued. Muhammad had to solve the problem by ordering the military leaders and his personal guard to split the plunder equally after this battle.[4]

Allah brought Muslims to the world to conquer and rule and populate the world. If any nation opposes the will of Allah and refuses to be Muslim, they will be the slaves of Muslims and pay tax to the Islamic authority. These nations are going to work hard, and you will benefit.[8]

THE FINAL REVELATION OF JIHAD: CONQUER THE WORLD

The last step in the development of jihad was when jihad stopped being regional and went worldwide. This change was based on a new Quranic verse received by Muhammad:

Fight them until there is no more *Fitnah* (disbelief and polytheism, i.e. worshipping others besides Allah) and the religion (worship) will be for Allah Alone [in the whole of the world].
—SURAH 8:39, THE NOBLE QURAN

As a result, Muhammad told his followers:

I heard the apostle of Allah say, I command by Allah to fight all the people till they say there is no god but Allah and I am his apostle. And whoever says that will save himself and his money.[9]

The Muslims put these revelations into practice right ay. They took jihad outside Arabia, attacking many untries in Asia, Africa, and Europe. This was the whole own world at the time.

In all Muhammad personally led twenty-seven battles. addition he sent out his army forty-seven times without (that's about seven times a year).[10] Muhammad's ended in AD 632 with his death. Despite his military

The invasion of Hunayn

Historian Ibn Hisham wrote in particular about invasion of Hunayn. The Muslim military lost due their hastiness to plunder the possessions of the er before the battle was finalized. When the Muslims after the possessions, the enemy ambushed them defeated them. Prophet Muhammad motivated hi tary by telling them, "Whoever kills someone is e to plunder his possessions."[5]

Hiring help for battle

Dr. Solomon Basheer mentions that Muhamn hired other tribes to help him fight, motivating tl a share of the plunder:

> Sometimes the Arabic tribes agreed to get iny with Muhammad and support him in tl tles. These tribes made contracts with the I leaders regarding what percentage of the they could take.[6]

This method of fund-raising con Muhammad's death. The second leader of ibn al-Khattab) is credited with many conq This leader also made agreements with othe for Islam.

> Jarir Bin Abdullah came and asked Muslim leader after the death of Muhar ibn al-Khattab), "If I go to Iraq wit to fight for Islam, can we keep 25 p plunder?" Umar agreed.[7]

Umar promised Muslims that they the people they conquered.

activity, he did not have a battle-related death. History records that he actually succumbed to an extended fever.

SUMMARY

After reviewing the culture and some of the characteristics of the Arabic people prior to Muhammad, we have a deeper understanding of the bloody history of Islam. Disagreements and misunderstandings often led to terrorist acts among the pre-Islam Arabic people due to their predisposition to act emotionally and violently as a whole.

Because Islam entitled them to the defeated enemies' possessions, the constant struggle for power among Arab tribes grew stronger and more brutal. Not only did they attack non-Muslims, but the early Muslim tribes also attacked each other. An example of this was the constant battle between the Ammoweyeen and the Hashemite, both of the tribe of Quraysh.

This culture readily accepted the philosophy of jihad that was revealed to Muhammad. These were progressive revelations of Quranic verses over a period of about twenty-two years. The progressive steps were:

1. Fight those who persecuted you (in Medina).

2. Conquer those who reject Islam in your region (the Arabian Desert).

3. Conquer the world in the name of Islam.

No Quranic revelation contradicted this final command of jihad, so it is still the goal of Islam today.

Chapter 9

THE ULTIMATE GOAL OF ISLAM

Worldwide Submission to Islam

JUST AS IN the days of Muhammad, the fundamentalist followers of Islam today are pursuing world conquest. The best way I can describe this mind-set is to let one of the leaders say it in his words.

One of the clearest writers and thinkers of modern jihad is Mawlana Abul Ala Mawdudi, the founder of Pakistan's fundamentalist movement. He has written many books and is one of Islam's most well-known scholars. The entire Islamic world considers him a leader who will be remembered throughout history. He explains the purpose of Islam as follows:

> Islam is not a normal religion like the other religions in the world, and Muslim nations are not like normal nations. Muslim nations are very special because they have a command from Allah to rule the entire world and to be over every nation in the world.[1]

He points out that the purpose of the strive is not about land, but about the religion—the goal is to subdue the world to the rule of Islam:

> Islam is a revolutionary faith that comes to destroy any government made by man. Islam doesn't look for a nation to be in better condition than another nation. Islam doesn't care about the land or who

owns the land. The goal of Islam is to rule the entire world and submit all of mankind to the faith of Islam. Any nation or power in this world that tries to get in the way of that goal, Islam will fight and destroy.

In order for Islam to fulfill that goal, Islam can use every power available every way it can be used to bring worldwide revolution. This is jihad.[2]

Mawdudi also expressed the idea that Islam is a political system and way of life that must replace all other ways of life:

Islam is not just a spiritual religion; Islam is a way of life. It is a heavenly system revealed to our world through the angel Gabriel, and the responsibility of Muslims is to destroy any other system in the world and to replace it with the Islamic system.

Everyone who believes in Islam in this manner can be a member of *Jamaat-i-Islami* [the Pakistani fundamentalist movement founded by the author]. I don't want anybody to think that Muslims who join the party of God are just normal Muslim missionaries or normal preachers in the mosque or people who write articles. The party of God is a group established by Allah himself to take the truth of Islam in one hand and to take the sword in the other hand and destroy the kingdoms of evil and the kingdoms of mankind and to replace them with the Islamic system. This group is going to destroy the false gods and make Allah the only God.[3]

By saying "false gods," the author is referring to political leaders who are not under Islamic authority, such as presidents or prime ministers of Western countries.

As you can see, Islam is the faith of struggle, revolution,

and war. Islam doesn't want a little piece of the world—it wants it all.

CHRISTIANS AS TARGETS

Christians are a target in the goal of world conquest because they resist conversion. This perspective is not just implied. It is explicitly stated.

In 1980 there was a meeting of the Muslim International World Society in Lehore, Pakistan. *Le Vigaro*, a prominent French newspaper, reported that the conference discussed ways that the Islamic world could end the existence of the Christian minority in the Muslim world or force them to become Muslim. Their timetable for achieving this was the end of the second millennium.

The chairman of this society sued the French newspaper in 1984, claiming that the report was false. But I believe the newspaper reported the truth, because that is truly the agenda of Islam.

Another example of the mind-set of converting Christians to Islam occurred during the Lebanese Civil War. This war between Christians and Muslims lasted twenty years, and no one could figure out how to get them to stop—not the United Nations or even the other Arab countries.

The late leader of Libya, Muammar Qaddafi, considered himself to be a great thinker, and he announced one day that he had a solution to the problem. His solution was for the Christians to convert to Islam and then they would be brothers and sisters with the Muslims and the fighting would stop. Qaddafi said:

> I hope there is a new generation of Lebanese Christians who will wake up one day and realize

Arabs cannot be Christians and Christians cannot be Arabs, so then they will convert to Islam and be true Arabs.[4]

METHODS OF JIHAD

We've seen that jihad was established in the Quran and that it involves world domination. Jihad is now the call for every Muslim. Now let us see how jihad is practiced in three stages in modern times.

Chapter 10

THE THREE STAGES OF JIHAD

How a Weakened Muslim Minority Takes Over

I F YOU LOOK at Muslim countries around the world, you will see that they are in one of the following three stages of jihad. (My source for these stages is Islamic theology based on the Quran.)

WEAKENED STAGE

This stage applies to Muslims when they are a weak, small minority living in a non-Islamic society. In this case overt jihad is not the call of the hour. Muslims submit to the law of the land, but they work to increase their numbers.

At this stage Muslims follow the word given to Muhammad in Mecca: "There is no compulsion in religion" (Surah 2:256, *The Noble Quran*). You have probably heard people in the media quoting this verse to prove that Islam does not compel, or force, anyone to convert.

Another key verse Muhammad received at this time was Surah 5:105:

> O you who believe! Take care of your ownselves. If you follow the (right) guidance [and enjoin what is right (Islamic Monotheism and all that Islam orders one to do) and forbid what is wrong (polytheism, disbelief and all that Islam has forbidden)] no hurt can come to you from those who are in error. The

return of you all is to Allah, then He will inform you about (all) that which you used to do.

—THE NOBLE QURAN

This verse was a response to Muslims in Mecca who were wondering what to do about all the unbelievers around them. It basically told them, "Be responsible for yourself. Don't worry about the infidels around you. You and they will all go before Allah one day and be judged by your works."

These verses speak of living quietly and at peace with unbelievers; however, we need to remember that Muhammad received these words when Muslims were a small, weak group in Mecca. After his movement gained strength, Muhammad received new words that canceled out (*naskh*) these verses.

PREPARATION STAGE

This stage is when the Muslims are a reasonably influential minority. Because their future goal is direct confrontation with the enemy, they make preparations in every possible area—financial, physical, military, mental, and any other area.

> Let not the Unbelievers think that they can get the better (of the godly): they will never frustrate (them). *Against them make ready your strength to the utmost of your power*, including steeds of war, to strike terror into (the hearts of) the enemies, of Allah and your enemies, and others besides whom you may not know, but whom Allah knows.
>
> —SURAH 8:59–60, ALI TRANSLATION,
>
> EMPHASIS ADDED

The Noble Quran includes some interesting commentary. Notice the words in parentheses:

> And make ready against them all you can of power, including steeds of war *(tanks, planes, missiles, artillery)* to threaten the enemy of Allah...
> —SURAH 8:60, EMPHASIS ADDED

This commentary should confirm for the reader that Muslims are practicing this verse in modern times.

JIHAD STAGE

This stage is when Muslims are a minority with strength, influence, and power. At this stage every Muslim's duty is to actively fight the enemy, overturning the system of the non-Muslim country and establishing Islamic authority.

This stage is based on the final revelation that Allah received concerning jihad, which is Surah 9:5. Though I quoted this verse earlier, it is so significant in Islamic thinking that it bears repeating:

> Fight and slay the Pagans wherever you find them, and seize them, beleaguer them, and lie in wait for them in every strategem (of war)...
> —ALI TRANSLATION

Muslims are commanded to kill anyone who chooses not to convert to Islam. The verse says "wherever you find them." There are no geographical limits.

MUHAMMAD'S EXAMPLE

These three stages are exactly what the prophet Muhammad lived out. At first he showed no animosity to his enemies (Phase 1). After he left Mecca, he spent his first year in

Medina preparing his army (Phase 2). Then he declared jihad, went back to fight his enemies, completely conquered Mecca, and brought it under his authority (Phase 3).

LEBANON

The recent history of the modern nation of Lebanon can provide us a good example of the three stages in practice.

Stage 1: Muslims cooperate with the Christian majority.

If you had visited Lebanon before their civil war, you would have seen the Hawaii of the Middle East. The capital, Beirut, was called the Paris of the Middle East. Lebanon was the most beautiful natural setting around.

The Muslim minority lived in harmony with the Christian majority. That was because the Muslims were a weak minority with no power. There were no talks about jihad, or holy war, those days in Lebanon.

Stage 2: Muslims get outside help to prepare for attack.

Slowly but surely in the 1970s the Islamic minority started the preparation stage by getting support from Libya on one side and Iran on the other. Not too long after that the Lebanese civil war began.

Stage 3: Muslims wage war against unbelievers.

The world watched as the beautiful country of Lebanon was divided into many pieces. Muslims denied any loyalty to their Christian brothers and sisters. They started militant groups that were after one goal—overturning the government and establishing an Islamic country.

One Islamic group was called Amal and was led by Nabih Bary; there was another Shiite group called Hizbollah, which was led by Sheikh Hassan Nasrallah.

Twenty years of war followed, but Muslims did not succeed in their mission.

Compromise (back to Stage 1)

Right now Lebanon has a secular government, but it has postponed presidential elections for two years now. The term of its Christian president, Michel Suleiman, ended in May 2014 and since then its Muslim prime minister, Tammam Salam, has been the acting president. There had been peace because Lebanon established a government that included all the warring parties. They even made the founder of Amal the president of the parliament and allowed Hizbollah to exist in South Lebanon because, they said, "We must have them there to defend against Israel." But now the world is watching to see whether the government upholds democracy or continues to move toward oligarchy, where a handful of men make decisions for the nation

JUSTIFYING DECEIT

The three stages of jihad show how circumstances are used to determine correct behavior. Another example of this in the Islamic mind set is the use of deceit. Islam justifies lying under certain circumstances. In the next chapter you will learn what those circumstances are and how they apply to jihad.

Chapter 11

WHEN LIES ARE JUSTIFIED

Deceit as a Part of War and to Avoid Trouble

MUSLIMS BELIEVE THAT war means deception, so lying is an important element of war in Islam. In this chapter we will look at the particular circumstances in which Muslims are permitted to lie.

LYING TO NON-MUSLIMS WHILE LIVING IN A NON-MUSLIM COUNTRY

Philosopher Ibn Taymiyah (1263–1328) wrote a book titled *The Sword on the Neck of the Accuser of Muhammad*. In it he described how Muslims should live in the weakened stage.

> Believers when in a weakened stage in a non-Muslim country should forgive and be patient with people of the book [i.e., Jews and Christians] when they insult Allah and his prophet by any means. Believers should lie to people of the book to protect their lives and religion.[1]

In other words, it's OK to lie to non-Muslims to protect yourself when you are a minority in their country.

There's a simple Islamic proverb that says, "If you can't cut your enemies' hand, kiss it."[2] This is clear in the prophet Muhammad's life and his teaching in Mecca and after. The peaceful lamb of Mecca, after immigrating to

Medina, became a roaring lion that threatened the whole Arabian Desert.

I never experienced living in the weakened state because Muslims are a strong majority in Egypt where I grew up. We Muslims practiced our beliefs in any way we liked. The Christians were the weakened minority. I never had a reason to lie to Christians, but I witnessed every day how these Christians lived under strong persecution as a minority in an Islamic country.

On the other hand, those practicing Islam in the United States, Canada, Europe, Australia, and South Africa are in the weakened stage. These Muslims are very good at presenting themselves as loving, caring, and forgiving people and claim to support democracy. They compromise any conflict between the image they want to present and what they truly believe.

They get along with Christians and Jews as if they were brothers. They present Islam to these countries as the answer to all humanity's problems. These Westernized Muslims present their religion as if it stands for mercy, freedom, fairness, and reconciliation. They portray Islam as a religion that does not show prejudice to any race or culture.

LYING ABOUT PEACE AGREEMENTS

Muslim groups will use peace talks or peace agreements to buy time so they can make new plans, prepare, and position themselves for victory. Muslim military leaders will tell the other side whatever it wants to hear in order to buy time, but when it comes time to deliver what is agreed on, you will see a different story.

Our modern history has witnessed many of these peace agreements that resulted in nothing happening. An example that comes to my mind is all of the agreements that took place between the Muslim groups in South Lebanon, the Hizbollah and Amal organizations. Another great example is the nine years of peace talks between Iraq and Iran, which resulted only in a vicious war.

I clearly remember what happened in Egypt during the fight between the government and the Islamic Group (*al-Gama'a al Islamiyya*). The leaders of the Islamic Group announced that they had suspended hostilities and were willing to meet at the negotiating table. That was nothing but buying time to regroup and go after the government even more than before. The Islamic Group used lies and tricks based on their understanding of the Quran and the prophet Muhammad's life teaching and history.

Many people may disagree with how I am portraying Islam; however, these facts are very clear in Islamic law. Let's see how Muhammad used lying, since his actions are part of the basis of Islamic law.

DENYING ISLAMIC FAITH

The first time the prophet Muhammad permitted denying Islam or him as a prophet was with Amar Ben Yasser.[5] Yasser, who was one of Muhammad's friends, was captured and held hostage by the tribe of Quraysh. The tribe tortured Yasser, so he denied Muhammad and Islam to gain freedom.

As soon as they set him free, he went back to Muhammad and confessed what had happened. Prophet Muhammad told Yasser that if that ever happened to him again he should do exactly what he did with no shame.

At a different time the prophet Muhammad heard that one of his enemies (Sha'ban Bin Khalid Al-Hindi) was preparing his troops to fight the Muslims. Muhammad sent Abdullah bin Anis Aljohani to assassinate this enemy. Aljohani asked the prophet Muhammad to describe the man he was supposed to kill. Muhammad told him to go and join the enemies' troops, curse Islam and Muhammad, and that he would find Al-Hindi that way.

Prophet Muhammad's messenger went to the enemies' camp. When he identified the leader, he struck up a conversation and cursed Muhammad and his people. To make a long story short, Aljohani was able to build a close enough relationship with his victim to cut off his head when he was sleeping. He brought the head to the prophet.

We see here that the prophet Muhammad's messenger used lying—denying the faith and cursing prophet Muhammad—in order to accomplish his mission.[4]

MUSLIMS DECEIVING OTHER MUSLIMS

When it comes to war, Muslims will even lie to other Muslims if necessary. This explains an incident between President Saddam Hussein of Iraq and President Hosni Mubarak of Egypt. Mubarak visited Hussein in Baghdad on the day before Iraq invaded Kuwait. Hussein promised Mubarak that he would not invade Kuwait, yet no sooner had Mubarak arrived home in Cairo than he heard that the invasion took place.

Hussein lied to his fellow Muslim, and he didn't even keep his word for twenty-four hours. That made the Egyptian president truly angry.[5]

GENERAL BELIEF ABOUT LYING

As you can see, Islam justifies and practices lying under war circumstances. The general attitude about lying can be illustrated by a story about one of Muhammad's favorite wives, Aiysha.

Lying is good if it is going to keep evil away.
Abi Hamid Al Gahazali (the founder of Sufism) states:

Know this that lying is not sin by itself, but if it brings harm to you it could be ugly. However, you can lie if that will keep you from evil or if it will result in prosperity.[6]

We know from Islamic history and the prophet Muhammad's autobiography that major jealousy took place between two of Muhammad's wives, Aiysha and Zeneb. Zeneb's sister started a rumor that Aiysha had an affair with another man.[7] Her motive was to help out her sister because the punishment for adultery in Islam is stoning.[8]

Aiysha denied having the affair, even though people close to the situation, including Muhammad's best friend, were sure she had done it. Lying was acceptable because it would keep the evil of stoning away.

SUMMARY

As you can see, lying and deceit are a part of the Islamic mind-set. This fact can be difficult for the Western mind to accept. Another difficult concept for the Western mind is the fact that a mosque is not just for religious activity. Mosques are used to support jihad, which was even made evident during the US bombing of Afghanistan.

Chapter 12

MUHAMMAD'S USE OF MOSQUES

House of Worship/House of War

URING THE US bombing campaign in Afghanistan, the US military bombed a mosque on October 23, 2001. The Lebanese News Center complained, "People who were praying inside were killed and injured."[1] On the other hand, the *Washington Post* said that, according to recent refugees, the Taliban had begun moving military equipment and personnel to mosques, schools, and other civilian sites to avoid attack.[2]

This incident illustrates two things: the use of deceit during war and the use of a mosque for war efforts.

A Mosque Isn't a Church

Most of the Muslims who are interviewed by Western media present Islam as a religion only. They emphasize the heart as the center of the Islamic teaching and the mosque as the worship place of the Muslims, just like a church or a synagogue.

However, the mosque during the prophet Muhammad's time was not just the place of worship. It was also a place to store weapons and make military plans. When Muhammad was in Medina, he used the mosque as head quarters for all his wars. Even after his death his successors used the mosques for the same purposes.

A mosque in Islam is the center for worship, justice, war

strategy, and government. This is because Islam is both a religion and government. Islam is a pen and a sword.

Prophet Muhammad made it clear to Muslims that the mosque isn't like a synagogue or a church. At his mosque in Medina (the second holiest site in Islam today), he planned his war strategy, held court, and received visiting tribal leaders. It was like the Pentagon, the White House, and the Supreme Court all in one place. The Islamic world was ruled from the mosque.

When there was an order to fight, the announcement was made at the mosque. The rulers after Muhammad continued this practice. Throughout Islamic history you can see that all movements of jihad came out of the mosque.

Egyptian Militants' Use of Mosques

In modern times mosques are still used as centers of war. The Egyptian Islamic groups are a good example. In 1986 the Egyptian police received orders from Zaki Bedr, prime minister of national security, to attack different mosques in southern Egypt because militant Islamic groups were using them.

The attack against the mosques caused much anger among moderate Muslims. The following dialogue occurred in the Egyptian Parliament between Bedr, who ordered the strikes, and the opposing party representative, Mohammed Mahfoz Helmy. Helmy explained why he was questioning Bedr's actions:

> The motive of my questions is not to accuse you of doing wrong, but as a representative of the people, we demand an explanation of the action of the administration of security in southern Egypt. The way that your administration surprised Muslim

worshipers inside of the mosque and arrested them was an insult to Islam.

Bedr answered by saying:

> We had accurate information that these radical Islamic groups used the mosque to plan and operate an attack on the citizens and the police. To be more specific, on Friday, October 31, 1986, we monitored the members of these groups taking weapons and people to the mosque to prepare for a major attack on the citizens of Assout and the police force. As a result of these attacks, six high-ranking officers and seventeen soldiers were wounded. However, we confiscated from the mosque many illegal handguns, and we found dead bodies of the citizens. We arrested fifty-seven members of these groups. After a short investigation we released two of these fifty-seven and jailed the other fifty-five.

The prime minister of national security told the Egyptian parliament that this wasn't the only time a mosque had been used as a military base. Five days before this invasion, another invasion was conducted.

> October 26, 1986, we received accurate information about a major plan for the Islamic radicals to destroy and attack the police and the citizens right after the Friday prayer. This information was enough for us to send out some of our best forces to stop these plans and keep national security under control. Moments after the arrival of the forces they discovered the gathering of 120 members of the Islamic Group inside the mosque. These members did not allow general worshipers to enter the

mosque to pray that day. We monitored them carefully and stood by to see how they would act. As soon as they made their first step to come out of the mosque and carry out their plans, we immediately attacked the mosque and arrested 121 people.

The prime minister of national security addressed the parliament by saying:

What these two incidents mean to me and my administration is that mosques are the gathering place and the centers for these radical Muslims. As long as I am in position, I will not tolerate it. We should stand together and unite in opinion to fight the threat of terrorism to our country even if they are raising the banner of Islam. I do not attempt to deny my responsibility for these attacks as my opponent's party claimed, but as a citizen of this great nation of Egypt I call the opponent's party to unite with our government and stand strong in the face of these threats of terrorism to keep our nation secure.[3]

What we saw in this documented modern history was that the Islamic Group movement (al-Gama'a al Islamiyya) used the mosque as a place of planning attacks and hiding weapons—following the example of the prophet Muhammad.

SECTION IV

THE DEVELOPMENT OF MODERN JIHAD

Chapter 13

FOREFATHERS OF TERRORISM

AD 600s to 1800s

YOU ARE ABOUT to embark on a guided tour through twelve hundred years of Islamic history. Along the way you will discover the events and movements that have produced the principles of jihad that are practiced today.

This chapter, which covers the time from Muhammad to the 1800s, will explain:

- The logic behind attacking leaders and governments who reject Islam, Muhammad, or the Quran

- Justification for killing women and children

- The belief that you should fight even if you know you will lose

- The suicide mission by Muhammad's grandson

- Eleventh-century terrorists who got high on marijuana before going to attack their enemies

GOOD REASONS TO KILL

Let's begin our tour by taking a few snapshots from the life of Muhammad. As you visualize these scenes from Muhammad's life, you may find it interesting to imagine what it would have been like if Jesus had behaved the same way.

When Muhammad moved to Medina in AD 622, he found many strong Jewish clans there who resisted him. The leader of a clan called Beni Nadir resisted with words. He excelled in poetry and its use in condemning Muhammad and his teachings.

This poetry got him in trouble with a powerful and competitive Jewish clan in the area (al-Aus), which had converted to Islam. (Yes, it's true; they converted.) When they heard this poetry, they planned to murder the author (Ka'b ibn al-Ashraf) in order to win the favor of Muhammad. They persuaded the poet's own brother to kill him. (Their mother was Jewish, but their father was Arabian.)

Because the clans were so competitive for Muhammad's favor, a rival Jewish clan that had also converted to Islam (al-Khazraj) looked for someone else Muhammad did not like in order to kill him as well. Abbah Rafah Salam was the second victim killed in order to keep Muhammad's favor.

In the meantime the prophet Muhammad ordered another man to go and kill a lady named Osama (daughter of Marawan), because she also used her poetry to condemn Muhammad and his teachings.[1]

The murder of the Jewish poet was perceived negatively among Arabs. Muhammad's first cousin, Ali ibn Abi Talib, who was among the first followers of Muhammad, assumed the responsibility of defending Muhammad's orders to murder. He told the people that God sent the angel Gabriel to Muhammad and commanded this man's death. Then he wrote a poem to confirm that this murder was God's command.

These three murders established a basic principle of behavior.

> **PRINCIPLE:** Anyone who conflicts with, disagrees with, or does not support Muhammad and his teachings should be killed.

MUHAMMAD PERMITS KILLING WOMEN AND CHILDREN

Let's see what the prophet of Islam said about killing women and children of the enemy.

Prophet Muhammad was once asked if it was OK to kill women and children of those who were polytheistic (believing in many gods) or infidels. He said, "I consider them as of their parents." In other words, if the parents were infidels, then it was permissible to kill their children.[2] Because the prophet of Islam believed this, this is what radical Muslims believe about killing women and children.

KILLING LEADERS WHO BREAK ISLAMIC LAW

Muhammad died in AD 632 after a long fever, according to historical records. The third leader to succeed him, Uthman ibn Affan, experienced much protest against his leadership and governing of the people. He was accused of mishandling money, moral failures, and other transgressions. A group of Muslims from many different nations surrounded his house and asked for his resignation. He swore by Allah that he would not respond to this threat and refused to give up leadership.

Within a few days they went back into the house and found him meditating and reading the Quran. They killed him there.

> **PRINCIPLE:** It is right to murder a governor or leader who is not in compliance with Islamic law.

After his death the Islamic nation was never the same. This was the fork in the road where the Islamic faith was divided forever.

FALSE TREATY CAUSES SPLIT BETWEEN MUSLIMS

After the murder of Islam's third leader, Muhammad's first cousin, Ali ibn Abi Talib, was chosen to be the fourth leader of Islam. Ali was revered by many because he was Muhammad's closest assistant, like his right arm.

The governor of El-Sham (Syria) opposed this appointment. He was from the same family as the previous leader who was murdered (Uthman). So the governor of El-Sham asked Ali to arrest the people who killed Uthman and judge them. Ali replied, "There are thousands; whom am I going to arrest? Whom am I going to judge?"

This started war. The governor, Muawiya ibn Abi Sufyan, fought many battles with Ali.

Ali's group became divided. Part of them opposed fighting and petitioned Ali to stop the war. They wanted to debate for a solution, choosing a representative from both sides who knew the Quran.

To make a long story short, Muawiya's representative presented Ali's representative with a deal to end the matter. The deal was that if Ali's followers removed Ali from leadership, the others would remove Muawiya from his leadership. Muslims could then elect whomever they saw fit according to the Quran.

Ali's followers kept their promise and removed Ali from leadership, but Muawiya's representative did not keep his promise. Instead, he declared Muawiya to be the only leader for the Muslims.

PRINCIPLE: Deceit is acceptable if it helps you achieve the goals of Islam.

MURDER OF ALI BY EL KHARIJ

By AD 660 the Islamic world was divided into two parties—those who followed Ali and those who followed Muawiya. Ali's followers were the Shiites, and Muawiya's followers were the Sunnis.

A new group splintered off from the Shiites. It was known as *el Kharij*. Just like jihad groups today, el Kharij called for reform. They wanted to practice Islam just as Muhammad did.

El Kharij decided the best plan of action would be to kill them all—Ali, Muawiya, and Muawiya's representative. By killing these three leaders they thought Muslims could go back to one leader, just as it was in the days of Muhammad.

One man was able to kill Ali even though Ali was held in great esteem among the Muslims. Immediately el Kharij's spiritual leader claimed a Quranic passage to justify what they did (Surah 2:204, 207).

The murder of Ali is a leading example of what many radical groups believe.

PRINCIPLE: When a government or a leader is found acting not in accordance with the Quran, Muslims have the right to declare them apostate and infidel. Islam's way of dealing with an apostate or infidel is killing.

This is another root of terrorism in the Islamic history. El Kharij principles and beliefs have been a terrorism threat to every empire, dynasty, society, or nation since then. The Islamic militia groups we see today around the world are a continuation of el Kharij. Because this ancient group was so influential, let's look at their beliefs.

EL KHARIJ BELIEFS

El Kharij is an Arabic word that means "one who goes out." In this part of Islamic history, el Kharij stepped out from under a leader or a government that they believed was not acting according to God's law and the Quran.

Here are some of their core beliefs:

- They believed that there is no law but God's law. They declared many imams (prayer leaders or Muslim preachers) to be infidels, including some of Muhammad's friends.

- They expected all Muslims to obey the call of jihad against rulers (Muslim or non-Muslim) who did not comply with the Quran. Anyone who did not participate in jihad was labeled an infidel.

- They believed in the right to kill children and women of infidels.

- They believed Muslims have the right to and control over women, children, and all material possessions of infidels.

- They made assassination, dishonesty, mistrust, and unfaithfulness a strong part of the Islamic faith.

Their beliefs have been demonstrated throughout the history of Islam.[3]

SUICIDE MISSION BY MUHAMMAD'S GRANDSON

After Muawiya's death in AD 680, his son Yazid assumed the leadership of the Islamic empire. As would be expected, he was not accepted by Ali's son, al-Husayn, who was leader of the Shiites at this time.

Al-Husayn felt that he should be the next leader of the Islamic empire. Not only was his father Muhammad's right arm and first cousin, but also his mother was Muhammad's daughter.

Al-Husayn knew that he didn't have enough people or weapons to defeat Yazid. However, he went to Iraq to fight him anyway. Al-Husayn was killed in a city called Kabala in the same year his father died.

The Shiites learned a new principle from the death of their leader.

PRINCIPLE: Fighting evil is a must; it does not matter if you win or you die. If you win, you will be honored by victory; If you die, you will be honored by God. Fighting evil is an honor either way.

Based on this belief, al-Husayn was a martyr of Islam. To this day he is held in high esteem and as a great example of self-sacrifice, especially among Shiite Muslims.

These beliefs give us a deeper understanding of why Muslims are willing to volunteer for suicidal attacks. They may not change much of the situation, but they get the opportunity to die as martyrs and heroes of Islam.

MARIJUANA WARRIORS

The name of this eleventh-century group is an Arabic description of people who smoke or eat hashish (derived from marijuana). *El-Hashashen* was a group of very religious Shiite Muslims who believed killing the enemy was an Islamic command to be martyred. This group was established in the eleventh century by a man named Hassan El-Sabaah.

Soldiers of this group used the drug hashish to get high before they went on suicide missions. While they were under the influence of the drugs, they visualized themselves in a garden with a many beautiful women. In their drug-altered states they got a little taste of what heaven would be like, so they rushed to do their jobs and get to the real thing.

This movement grew quickly and accomplished a great number of assassinations and murders all over Persia and Iraq. The members of this group assassinated many military leaders and government officials of the Sunni Muslims. In the beginning of the twelfth century the El-Hashashen movement almost spread over the entire Middle East region. Not one ruler or governor was safe from their harassment.

IBN TAYMIYAH AND NO TOLERANCE

At the beginning of the fourteenth century a powerful Sunni leader came on the scene—Ibn Taymiyah. Born in a Syrian city named Haran in 1263 (661 AH), he fought the Mongolian invasion of Syria (1299–1303). Ibn Taymiyah taught that Mongolian Muslims were not true Muslims and that his countrymen should not submit to their authority. He also declared that anyone who submitted to them, helped them, or dealt with them was just like them—infidels. From this point on Ibn Taymiyah acted as if he were a military leader, declaring many Muslims to be infidels and attacking them.

Ibn Taymiyah established the mind-set of no tolerance. He reinforced principles that were also practiced centuries earlier.

> **PRINCIPLE:** Muslims should resist, fight, and overturn any Islamic government that doesn't govern the land according to the Islamic law only.

> **PRINCIPLE:** Muslims should enforce jihad on anybody whose beliefs differ from Islam, especially Jews and Christians.

We have seen a great deal of Ibn Taymiyah's influence for the last two centuries on most of the Islamic movements. Today's terrorism is a result of this mind-set.

WAHHABI MOVEMENT

Based on the same foundation that Ibn Taymiyah established, Muhammad ibn Abd al-Wahhab (1703–1792) led the Wahhabi movement. This movement resisted, fought, and overturned the Turkish government. Abd al-Wahhab established a new 100 percent Islamic nation, which eventually became Saudi Arabia.

The royal family of Saudi Arabia in power today are the descendants of Abdul Aziz Bin Saud, the political leader who worked with Wahhab to establish the nation of Saudi Arabia. At the same time the Saudi government is also facing an el Kharij movement, those who would like to go back to the original principles. Osama bin Laden was an example of someone from that group.

Ibn Taymiyah's mind-set has influenced our world today in a great way. Many movements are now trying to overturn their governments and go back to the teaching of Muhammad with no tolerance or compromise. They are pursuing their mission with military force. History is definitely repeating itself.

SUMMARY

Now that you have seen the historical roots of terrorism starting with Muhammad and going through the 1800s, we come to the man I refer to as the founding father of modern jihad. He was put to death by the government of Egypt for his teaching, and many of his books are banned in Egypt and other countries, including Libya and Iraq. Yet his influence lives on. His name is Sayyid Qutb.

Chapter 14

THE FOUNDING FATHER
OF MODERN JIHAD

Sayyid Qutb: From the Village to the Gallows

THE 1920s WERE an exciting time in the history of many Middle Eastern countries. Many were finally liberated from the authority of the Europeans—some from the British, some from the French, some from the Italians, and some from the Turkish—or they were on their way to liberation. One of these countries was Egypt.

For first time in history Egypt had a president. The people of Egypt were finally starting to see the light of freedom again, many for the first time in their lifetimes.

Events in Turkey would soon propel Egypt toward Islamic fundamentalism. In 1924 the Turkish military leader Mustafa Kemal Ataturk established a thoroughly secular state in Turkey. In doing so, he overturned the Islamic succession system that had led the Islamic world for six hundred years. In effect he threw out the Muslim system and replaced it with a Westernized, military system.

Muslims reacted negatively to this, including Muslims in Egypt. In response a spiritual leader named Sheikh Hassan al-Banna started the Muslim Brotherhood Movement in Egypt. This is what we will refer to as el Kharij all over again. His beliefs were a mixture of early el Kharij, El-Hashashen, and the mind-set of Ibn

(Courtesy of Sinai Publishing, Cairo, Egypt)

Sayyid Qutb, the "Martin Luther" of the modern jihad movement, put to death by the Egyptian government because of his book *Signs Along the Road.*

Taymiyah. His goal for Egypt was to reapply the Islamic law and to reestablish an Islamic succession system.

The Muslim Brotherhood was very militant, aggressive and full of hatred toward the leadership of the country and anyone who would not comply with Islamic law. They used terrorist methods to shake up society and pursue their agenda of bringing back the original glory of Islam.

After Israel was established as a nation in 1948, radical fundamentalist groups flourished even more. The establishment of Israel marked the beginning of many wars between the Jews and the Arabs.

The fundamentalist groups created many cells of rebellious, hateful Muslims who were willing to die for their cause. Their animosity was not directed at the Jews alone. They taught their followers that the leaders of Egypt and the rest of the Arabic world were not true Muslims.

They aggressively taught that Islamic law should be applied with zero tolerance for government interference or for people of any other faith. These militant and extreme terrorist groups focused their activities on assassination. In their minds killing was the only way to make Islamic nations resubmit to the Quran and the Islamic law.

In 1948 the Muslim Brotherhood assassinated Egyptian Prime Minister Mahmoud Nokrashy Pasha. In 1949 they attempted the assassination of the new prime minister of Egypt, Ibrahim Abdel Hadi, but instead they killed Supreme Court Judge Moustashar Ahmad El-Kazendari.

In this atmosphere an intelligent young Egyptian finished his degree and began a promising career in education. Sayyid Qutb, who was born in 1906 in Southern Egypt, was chosen by the government to come to the United States in 1948 to study special methods of education. After he returned to Egypt from his trip to the United States he joined the Muslim Brotherhood movement.

VISITING AMERICA—AND HATING IT!

This was Qutb's first time ever outside of Egypt. He came back from America filled with both envy and hostility toward the United States. The following is a quote from a letter he sent to a friend while in the United States.

> Nowhere else on earth could I find people that excel in education, knowledge, technology, business and civilization like the Americans. However, the American values, ethics and beliefs are below the standard of a human being.

When Qutb was in the United States, he spent time in Washington, DC, California, and Colorado. He was very impressed by America's natural beauty, great size, educational institutions, and diversity of population. Yet he felt that America's resources were wasted on materialism.

> It seems to me that there is no relation between greatness of culture and greatness of the people that create this culture. It is obvious that Americans have focused all of their ingenuity on the production of materialism, but they don't have much to offer as to what makes humans great.

He was disgusted with what he saw as a lack of religious conviction.

> No one else in the world has built more churches than the Americans.... You will find Americans in church on Sundays, Christmas, Easter and special religious occasions, yet they are so empty and do not have a spiritual life. The last thing that an American would think about in everyday life is their religion.

Qutb was also angry because American influence had led the Muslim world astray from the ways of Islam.

> Not only the non-Muslim world is pagan and heathen but also the existing Muslim world is so influenced by the rest of the world.[1]

QUTB'S KEY BELIEFS

Sayyid Qutb, the founding father of modern jihad, authored more than seven books. However, the book that earned him a death sentence from the Egyptian government at the age of fifty-nine can only be found on the black market. The name of that book is *Signs Along the Road (Ma'alim fi el-Tareek)*. The Egyptian government arrested Qutb and sentenced him to death in 1965 during the presidency of Gamal Abdel Nasser. The Egyptian government thought that by killing Qutb they could stop the mind-polluting philosophy he taught.

The Egyptian government ordered the police to take into custody and burn any copies of his book; however, copies survived. I read this book in Egypt before I left. The book's contents continue to be distributed through the radical Muslims in Egypt and throughout the Islamic world.[2]

Sayyid Qutb and *Signs Along the Road* have become the heartbeat of the radical Islamic movements of today. Some of the better known groups in Egypt that follow his teaching are *al-Jihad, al-Takfir wal-Hijra* (Repentance and Holy Flight), *El Najune Min El-Narr* (Rescued from Hell), and many other terrorist groups. Qutb is the philosopher and spiritual leader of today's Islamic terrorist groups.

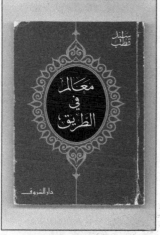

(Courtesy of Shorouk International, Cairo, Egypt)

Signs Along the Road, the book that earned Qutb the death sentence but continues to guide jihad movements today.

Let's take a closer look at Qutb's beliefs.

Qutb felt that the world had regressed to the way it was before Muhammad's teachings—pagan and idolatrous.

> Today we are living like heathens—just like the days before Islam in the way people act, the world's culture and what they believe and think. It is all heathenism. Even in the Islamic world, Muslims' education, their philosophies, their culture, their thinking and their laws are all far from the true Islam.[3]

Qutb believed that Allah is the only ruler over earth and that no human should rule or govern the earth. Therefore, he rejected all man-made systems of government, including democracy, socialism, dictatorships, and communism. He wrote:

The way that life is lived today is an insult to Allah and his authority on earth. It contradicts godly principles. This idolatrous world gives the authority of Allah to humans as if they were God. We have become our own gods. These heathens are not like the ones before Islam, but far worse. Today's heathens reverence and honor man-made constitutions, laws, principles, systems and humanistic methods. They disregard Allah's law and his constitution for life.[4]

Qutb believed Muslims should rebel and resist any human power on earth until they overturn all man-made governments. This is the ultimate calling for a Muslim, and it is not to be compromised, deviated from, or stopped.

We should immediately eliminate this pagan influence and the heathen pressure on our world. We must overturn this current society with its culture and leadership of infidels. This is our first priority: to shake and change the foundations of heathens. We must destroy whatever conflicts with true Islam. We should get out from under the bondage of what keeps us from living in the ways that Allah wants us to live.[5]

His logic was as follows: good and evil cannot live together, truth and false are not the same, and people cannot live under the authority of both man and God. And to please God, people should destroy the ways of man. He wrote:

Demolish all governments and organizations that are established by man. Eliminate human racism that exalts one over the other. The return of God's kingdom can only be established by a movement of power and the sword.

Qutb, following the teaching of Ibn Taymiyah, went as far as declaring some Islamic leaders to be apostate infidels. He felt that this declaration gave him support from other Muslims and from Allah.

Qutb not only applied these methods within his country, but he also called the movement to enforce his beliefs all over the world.

PROFILE OF A JIHAD GROUP

In his book Qutb brought the reader to an important question: How can this revolution be accomplished? He did not specify exactly what should be done to accomplish this. Perhaps he feared the Egyptian government would see this book as a plan for a new Islamic revolution to overturn their government.

Or perhaps he feared the government would be angry with him because his thinking was so similar to Sheikh Mawlana Abul Ala Mawdudi, the leader of the Islamic movement in Pakistan. (This is the author whose words I used earlier to define jihad.)

However, an average reader who can read between the lines would conclude that Qutb envisioned the following type of group to carry out the call of Islam:

- This group would be purified from any and all inclination to lean toward the pagan world. They would eliminate all sources of spiritual beliefs that would compete with Allah and the Quran. This includes destroying books and man-made Islamic commentaries.

- They would accept no authority but Allah for beliefs, worship, systems, laws, and constitution.

- They would experience tremendous resistance from the rest of the world. Existing governments and authorities would cause them financial difficulties. Their families and society would reject them.

- They would claim that the new Islamic world could exist only if their group obtained a great deal of power and force to gain the respect and submission of the pagan world. They would use armed forces to overthrow governments, just as Muhammad did.

- There would be no mercy or compromise in this war.

- This Muslim group may have a difficult start, but as soon as true believers hear the call, the numbers will multiply to hundreds, thousands, tens of thousands, and then throughout the world.

"Defeated" Muslims

Qutb was very frustrated with Muslims who questioned the call to jihad as a command to be followed by all Muslims of all time. Qutb asserted:

The order in which Allah gave Islam to Muhammad was gradual and progressive to maximize positive results toward Islam. Many Muslims take the early verses of this progression of teaching out of context as if they are Allah's final and complete instructions. These Muslims strip Islam of its power and build their own theory on these verses.

The results of this type of interpretation of Islam are Muslims who are living a defeated life spiritually and mentally. They are under the pressure of the hopelessness that they cannot spread Islam any longer.

These people are only Muslims by name. They only have the title of Islam but not the power. They only fight to defend their beliefs.

These are the same Muslims who like to carry the title of Islam without the responsibility of overturning the entire earth with all of its politics and earthly governments. These Muslims choose to compromise the message of Islam by not forcing high taxes on people who refuse the message of Islam.[6]

Qutb expressed deep frustration about the people whom he described as "defeated Muslims, spiritually and mentally." He complained about them distorting the meaning of jihad. "These Muslims write about jihad in Islam as just a spiritual jihad against evil." He said that the truth is:

Islam is nothing but Allah declaring his liberation to the human race on earth from slavery. Allah declares his lordship over the entire earth. This means that Allah greatly protests all man-made government and authorities. Absolute rebellion is a must against anything on earth that conflicts with Islam. We should eliminate and destroy with great power anything that stops Allah's revolution.[7]

WORDS BACKED BY ACTION

Following Qutb's philosophy, the Muslim Brotherhood attempted to kill Egyptian President Gamal Abdel Nasser twice—once in 1954 and once in 1965. These terrorists planted bombs in many different places of gathering. Bombs were planted in the Cairo Bab El-Kalk Court and many police stations. They murdered many Egyptian policemen.

To defend itself, the Egyptian government placed many of the leaders of these groups in prison. Many of them left the prison in their coffins without a trial. President Nasser ordered the guards just to shoot them.

Sayyid Qutb's execution by the Egyptian government elevated his writings to a level of great authority in the Islamic world. He is respected and known by radical Muslims all over the world. He is held in esteem by Muslims the same way John Calvin or Martin Luther is held in esteem by Christians. There were long-term effects not only in Egypt, but also in the entire world.

Chapter 15

THE PHILOSOPHERS OF JIHAD

More Books That Guide Today's Terrorists

T HERE IS A pattern among the philosophers of jihad. An author will write a book outlining his ideas of jihad and how it should be carried out. He will gather a following. Then that author is put to death by the government of his own country. The dead author is a hero, and his books gain more power.

Then the next author comes along and builds on the same ideas, only making them more radical. After three or four of these cycles we have the philosophy of jihad today that resulted in al Qaeda and the attack on the United States on September 11, 2001.

DR. SALAH SEREA: THE EGYPTIAN ISLAMIC LIBERATION MOVEMENT

Qutb's teaching and philosophy captured a large number of Muslims, though many of his followers were imprisoned at the time of his hanging. Following this period of time a man named Dr. Salah Serea led a new radical movement called the Islamic Liberation Movement (*Hezb al-Tarir*). He based his movement on the mind-set of Qutb's teaching. His goal was to overturn the Egyptian government and declare a new Islamic nation. Let's look at what Dr. Serea had to say:

- Muslims are nothing but talk. They make commitments but do not follow through. Throughout the last few centuries, Islam changed from a religion of action to a religion of just talk.

- The priority of the Islamic nations should be to carry on the message of Islam and apply it internally and externally in all ways.

- Jihad should be enforced. It is the way of paying a price for what you stand for and keeping the message alive. It should be practiced inside the nation and carried out to the world.

- Our goal is to find out the most effective way to overturn and destroy any governments that do not completely comply with Islamic law, including existing Muslim countries.

- We will establish a great Islamic nation that will stretch across the world. The only political system will be Islamic law.[1]

Serea felt that leaders of the Muslim world are corrupted because they enforce fasting and prayer but not jihad:

Many of the rulers of the Islamic world today are people of prayer. They have built mosques. They have reinforced fasting and prayer, and they do whatever it takes to have the appearance of good Muslims. Their ulterior motive is to gain popularity using the religious sincerity of the Muslims. Meanwhile they carefully keep true Islam away from the hearts of the people. They persecute anyone who stands for true Islam with physical violence. These rulers are infidels, and anyone who stands behind them or supports them is also an infidel.[2]

Dr. Serea continued to complain about what he saw as the corruption of the existing Islamic governments by saying that Islam is one of the laws they use to govern the land when it should be the only law used to govern. Dr. Serea stated:

They are building mosques, but they are also building places of secular entertainment. They are broadcasting the Quran and also music and dancing. They give to charities and are also gambling. What is popular among these Muslims is only the worship part of Islam, and they leave out jihad, the heartbeat of Islam. These Muslims carefully read the Quran daily, and many of them cry in their prayers, but they do not go out and carry on the mission of Islam through jihad. These are hypocrite infidels. They are the shame of Islam.[3]

Dr. Serea practiced what he preached. On April 19, 1974, Dr. Serea and his movement launched their offense against the Egyptian government. They invaded a military training institute in Cairo, hoping to establish a base from which to overturn the government.

The Egyptian authorities responded with great force and arrested him and all the members of his movement. In October 1975 the federal government of Egypt sentenced Dr. Serea and many of his followers to death; twenty-nine followers of the movement remained in prison.

Egypt and the Islamic world were just entering a new

episode of terrorism and radical Islamic groups. Even before Dr. Serea was sentenced, a new radical group was birthed in Egypt.

SHOKRI MOUSTAFA

Al-Takfir wal-Hijra (Repentance and Holy Flight) was the next militant group to carry on the goals of Dr. Serea. Its founder was Shokri Ahmad Moustafa, who was from the same region of Egypt as Sayyid Qutb. Born in 1942 Shokri Moustafa was only twenty-four years old when Qutb, the father of modern jihad, was hanged. He was thirty-three years of age when Dr. Serea was sentenced to death.

(Courtesy of Shorouk International, Cairo, Egypt)
Shokri Moustafa, put to death by the Egyptian
government in 1977 for jihad activity.

Shokri Moustafa was clear on what his goals and priorities were. The following is what he stated before the Egyptian federal court in the session on November 7, 1977:

My greatest priority, for which I am willing to pay whatever price is required to accomplish it, is to see a true Islamic movement take off. I must find fertile ground to plant a great Islamic nation worldwide. I will revive Islam and bring it to its original state.

The danger that the Egyptian court faced with Moustafa was that he had a large number of members in his organization who would obey him at a moment's notice. Moustafa said:

Each member of our movement would be willing to sacrifice his own life to fulfill the responsibility that Allah has put on our shoulders. That responsibility is to spread the message of Islam across the earth and reinforce it with the sword. My group of people will fight with me to the end to accomplish the great mission.

Shokri Moustafa kept a journal of poems in his own handwriting that the court used in his conviction. (Poetry is deeply ingrained in Islamic culture.) In Moustafa's most popular journal *The Battle (El-Maalhamma)* we find the poem "Before the Flood," which was written in 1967. In it Moustafa expressed his deep sorrow and frustration with the current Muslim existence. He told himself that he must prepare for the calling on his life and his mission, and in doing so he should prepare to meet Allah.

In another poem titled "Immigration" ("*El-Hejhera*") we see his belief that everything on this earth is vanity and that he simply wants to accomplish his mission and leave this earth.

In another journal titled *Expectation (El-Tawaseemat)* he asked, "Where is the mother of the villages?" This is what Mecca was called during the time of Islam. Mecca is the city where Muhammad was persecuted, so it is considered evil for doing that. Moustafa was saying that Egypt was the modern Mecca, the modern persecutor of Islam. He called Egypt the place that imports evil, blasphemy, and error. "It is the country of infidels," he wrote.

Moustafa comforted himself by saying, "Just as Muhammad left Mecca and immigrated to Medina to establish the first Islamic nation, I too will mentally escape from Mecca to go to my Medina to begin again."

From Egypt Moustafa planned to start an Islamic nation that would go all over the world. First he planned on winning many people from his home country, which would be the foundation for building a worldwide Islamic nation. From this new foundation he would export Islam to the world.

One of Moustafa's most disturbing beliefs was that his quest to spread Islam would involve great tension between the East and the West, which would lead to a worldwide nuclear war.[4] He believed that most of the world would be destroyed during this war, but his followers would not be killed because they would hide in caves of remote, isolated mountains. After the desolation, his followers would emerge from the caves, inherit the earth, and rule it by the sword.

He believed that the use of the sword as a primary weapon, as it was in the time of Muhammad, would come back as a result of all modern technology and existing weapons being destroyed in a nuclear war.

MOUSTAFA'S DEFENSE

Shokri Moustafa's movement wanted to make Qutb's philosophy a reality. The members of this organization planned to start by living in complete isolation from the society of heathen. They were planning to work hard to increase their numbers and prepare for the point of power that would enable them to overturn the government and establish an Islamic nation. They believed their mission would be accomplished in two phases:

- Phase I—The absolute destruction of the heathen world

- Phase II—Muslims would inherit the earth and everything on it

During the prosecution of Moustafa, the Egyptian court asked him from what source he drew his philosophy. Moustafa replied, "It is from the clear-cut source of the Quran and Allah's word. We don't know anything, but Allah knows everything. We must learn only from Allah, and Allah only speaks from the Quran." He based this on the Quranic verse:

Allah knows but you do not know.
—Surah 2:216, The Noble Quran

Any books other than the Quran are not acceptable.

Moustafa explained that this was what Allah said, and he asked the Egyptian Islamic authority if they were going to reject what the Quran says.

Shokri Moustafa and his organization were on trial for the kidnap and murder of a professor at Al-Azhar University—Dr. Husein El-Thehaby, one of the icons of the university. He was targeted because he led a team of professors to condemn and stop Moustafa's movement.

Moustafa considered him to be an enemy of Allah and one of the infidels who were taking the side of the government.

Addressing the Egyptian court, Moustafa said that because Dr. El-Thehaby sold out to the pressure of the Egyptian government and compromised Allah's word to please man, they had carried out Allah's judgment against this apostate infidel.

Shokri Moustafa's movement gained more ground after a meeting between the Egyptian media and a new team from Al-Azhar University. Dr. Sayed El-Tawhel, a professor of Islamic studies at Al-Azhar, led this new team, which advised, "Don't judge this group. They are sincere Muslims who just want to bring back the glory of Islam. We just need to sit down and talk with them." This statement was to clarify the air in Egypt and stop the confusion about a media broadcast that said Moustafa's organization was trying to spread a new Islam that was not based on the Quran.

The main Egyptian newspaper issued a statement from Dr. El-Tawhel, warning Al-Azhar University authorities not to issue any statements or judgments in the name of Islam against Moustafa. He called them to go back to the Quran and read it with new eyes; they would see that Moustafa's group was made up of sincere Muslims loyal to the call of Islam. Dr. El-Tawhel commended Moustafa and his group, saying that his heart's desire was to see more and more young people like them. He said that the Islamic world today needed people like them to lead it back to true Islam.[5]

THE EXECUTION AND THE BOOK

Shokri Moustafa was sentenced to death. He left behind a radical group that did not believe in any kind of submission, leadership, or respect for the existing government in Egypt or the rest of the world.

His death confirmed to them that these governments were heathen. They believed every word when he said that these governments were infidels and any one who submits to them would be just like them.

Moustafa left behind a book with all of his beliefs and philosophies. The book is called *The Leader (Al-Kalafa)*. The Egyptian government confiscated every single copy that they could find and burned them. The actions of the government increased the value of this book among the followers of Muslim radical groups, which to this day continue distributing his beliefs and teaching.

Moustafa's new twist

This book was full of the mind-set of Qutb's teaching. The only new twist that made Moustafa more dangerous than Qutb is that he wanted to start by attacking religious institutes, police, and military institutes. Moustafa explained that they should attack the religious institutes because they have submitted to the authority of a heathen government, which conflicts with Islamic law. He said to attack police and military institutes because they protect heathen governments and enforce their laws. The police and military

(Courtesy of Shorouk International, Cairo, Egypt)

Shokri Moustafa appearing before the Egyptian court.

institutes are the powers that persecute, imprison, and kill true Muslims.

Moustafa's book declared there was not much difference between the existing governments of Israel, the United State, and European countries. They are all heathen and the enemy of Allah according to Moustafa, and they should be fought through jihad until they submit to Islam completely.[6]

In 1977 when the Egyptian government carried out the death sentence on Moustafa and some of his leadership, they were thinking that it would be the end of the movement. This was not the case. Radical groups flourished in Egypt in the 1970s and 1980s due to a variety of reasons. It was all leading to another attempt to overthrow the government.

Chapter 16

RECRUITING FOR HOLY WAR

Terrorist Group Controls Egyptian Universities

N THE EARLY 1970s the Egyptian government released many of the members of the Muslim Brotherhood Movement from the prisons. President Sadat thought that their activity would counteract the influence of the Soviets and communism in Egypt, which it did. But at the same time the movement expanded, gained power, and became dangerous to the Egyptian government as well.

A new group called *al-Gama'a al-Islamiyya*, known as the Islamic Group Movement, or IGM, in English, was formed. Its strategy was to recruit and disciple young men from the high schools and colleges.

Many of the older generation that were released from the prisons worked as mentors for the new generation. These mentors were former professors from Al-Azhar University.

RECRUITING AT MY UNIVERSITY

When the new Islamic Group Movement started, its leaders followed the first two steps of Qutb's plan. They started camps all over to prepare their members spiritually and mentally. They filled their camps with recruits from the universities of Egypt. These groups had complete control of the campuses of the major universities in Egypt. The routine of the camps was for new members to come in for three to seven days to pray, fast, and study the Quran and the history of Islam. They focused their study on Muhammad's life and how he led jihad and applied the Islamic law. The leaders of these groups brainwashed the students to believe that they were the only hope of Islam and that it was the time to get Islam back on the right track toward establishing an Islamic nation worldwide.

At the time I was living in Al-Azhar dorm in Nasser City in Cairo. This dorm had thirty-five hundred students from all over the country.

The Islamic Group Movement members utilized the campus mosque for their daily prayers, and in between prayers they worked hard to recruit and disciple new students into the movement. One day we were all at the mosque for prayer when an IGM leader stood up and said, "There is a secret Christian group that rents apartments near the dormitories. They are against Islam, and they are forcing female students to have sex with Christian men." Then he gave them the apartment numbers. The students were shocked and emotionally boiling.

He continued, "There is also a little shop near the entrance to the girl's dormitory. It is selling pens, paper, and snacks. This shop is distributing pornography magazines for free to the Muslim girls. This Christian group is trying to get the girls out of Islam."

A fire was lit in the heart of every student. "Christians! Doing this to our girls? We will go and destroy them!"

Hundreds of students stampeded to the shop. They doused it with gas and burned it to the ground. Then they went to the apartments and destroyed them too.

The mob of students returned to the dorm at lunchtime but refused to eat. They destroyed thirty-five hundred meals and kicked the workers out of the building. Then they locked the doors and rioted, running around the building shouting, *"Allah o akbar!"* (Allah is great!)

For three days the dormitory was locked down. There was no eating, no going to classes. But some students did not support this movement. To escape, they had to scale the wall around the dormitory and run back to their homes. I was one of those students. The standoff did not end until the president of the university and a government secretary met with the leader of IGM at the university.

Later the minister of national security came to campus and declared that no Christian group was seducing the female students. This helped many students to recognize that groups like the IGM were just violent people who were trying to create an enemy to fight. They just wanted to show their power to society.

SPIRITUAL LEADERSHIP

Once a year the movement organized national rallies. The different university campuses united to hear people such as Sheikh Abed Al-Hamid Kishk, Sheikh Omar Abdel Rahman, or other leaders and icons of Islam inspire the movement. Year after year this movement spread its wings over Sudan, Tunisia, Algeria, Yemen, Syria, Iraq, Lebanon, and many other countries.

Sheikh Kishk and Sheikh Abdel Rahman made an incredible impact on the minds of the young men during that time.

Sheikh Abed Al-Hamid Kishk

Sheikh Abed Al-Hamid Kishk was one of the most eloquent leaders of Islam in Egypt and the Arab world. Sheikh Kishk had a very aggressive voice and special talent of utilizing the old classical Arabic language to hold the audience in the palm of his hand. He used his talents to deliver many political messages to thousands of young, thirsty minds. He controlled the minds of the audience almost like magic; he made them cry and laugh in the same breath.

Kishk was well known for his impudent and sassy tongue, and he attacked the government and those in high positions many times. Sheikh Kishk used cassette tapes to invade the Arabic world, breaking all the geographic barriers with his radical messages.

Sheikh Omar Abdel Rahman

Sheikh Abdel Rahman was my professor for "freshman Quran" at Al-Azhar. He is now serving a life sentence in the United States for the 1993 bombing of the World Trade Center. But before he came to the United States, he had an even greater impact on the Middle East.

As a graduate and professor of Al-Azhar University, he has his doctorate of philosophy in interpretation of the Quran and Islamic law. Sheikh Abdel Rahman became the spiritual authority and leader for today's radical groups.

His leadership was the perfect model for these radical terrorist groups as seen in the following characteristics:

- He did not compromise the Quran.

- He did not have any relationship with the government and did not submit to its laws and authority.

- He was a teacher of the Quran and Islamic law, which made many young Muslims trust him and obey his commands, even to kill.

- He led jihad according to the Quran and believed in building an Islamic nation according to Islamic law. He was willing to give his life for the cause.

While these two men were recruiting and building support to overturn Egypt, another nation in the Middle East actually succeeded in doing so. It would provide inspiration and support for many radicals. This country was Iran.

Chapter 17

INSPIRED BY IRAN

A Truly Islamic State Is Born

N 1979 IRANIAN Shiite Muslims started their Islamic movement. They were against Muhammad Reza Shah Pahlavi and his government. The spiritual leaders of the country supported this movement to overturn the government.

Prior to this time fundamentalist Iranian Muslims did not express their beliefs. They were in tremendous fear of the government. They followed the *Al-Tokiya* method of hiding their faith: "Inside I hate you, but outside I pretend to be your friend." *Al-Tokiya* meant that the Muslims behaved in a way that pleased the government, not according to their beliefs.

The rebellion started after many of the Shiite Muslims regained the spirit of martyrdom that was buried inside of them. They remembered how al-Husayn, the son of Ali ibn Abi Talib and the grandson of Muhammad, went to fight his enemy even though he knew he would be killed. The Iranian spiritual leaders reminded the Shiites of the history of martyrdom. Immediately Iranian Muslims started to abandon *Al-Tokiya* and to adopt the spirit of Shiite martyrdom.

At the same time and from a distance Ayatollah Khomeini was leading this movement through cassettes. From a French village called Le Château, Khomeini recorded on cassette tapes his teaching, beliefs, and plan for the new Islamic revolution and sent them to the people of Iran. These cassettes brainwashed millions of people. An Italian writer wrote a book about the Iranian revolution and called it *The War of Cassettes*.

Thousands of Iranians were killed in this revolution. Iranian history had never recorded such a powerful revolution before.

The revolution overthrew the government and succeeded in establishing an Islamic government. Ayatollah Khomeini was flown from France back to Iran. He bowed down twice outside the aircraft before the flight to Tehran and thanked Allah. Through reporters and media he sent a message to the Shiites in Iran and to the world that "no one can defeat a nation that receives Allah's orders and obeys them."

Millions of Iranians received him at his arrival at Tehran's airport. The city was shaken by the sound of them shouting, *"Allah o akbar!"*—Allah is great. They carried Khomeini on their shoulders all the way to a graveyard called *Al-Ferdose*, where all the martyrs of the revolution were buried. Khomeini stated, "No more *Al-Tokiya* after today." He meant that the Shiite Muslims now had the power to practice their beliefs with no fear of a government or any other power in this world.

REACTION AT THE UNIVERSITY

Those historical days had a great impact on Islam and the world. At the university members of the Islamic Group Movement used what happened in Iran to rebel against the Egyptian government. They violently protested classes in all universities in Egypt, including Al-Azhar University.

Thousands of students shouted out in support of

Khomeini. This protest included great numbers of students who had never been a part of the Islamic Group Movement before. This occasion was a great opportunity for new recruits.

The protest snowballed out of control throughout Egypt. The number of the protesters grew to be a major threat to the Egyptian authorities.

The Islamic Group members led thousands to shout against the government. They declared that Islam should take over Egypt, just like in Iran. "Oh Sadat, oh you coward, you are the puppet of the Americans," they shouted.

They cried out against the nation of Israel too: "Patience, patience, all ye Jews: Muhammad's military is on their way back to you."

IRAN EXPORTS ITS REVOLUTION

The Iranian revolution supported many Islamic radical groups in the Arab nations and around the world. The leadership of the Iranian revolution said they were getting into a new business. They were going to export their best product to the entire world—true Islamic law and revolution.

In the years since the revolution Iran has supported all of the Islamic fundamentalist groups that have terrorized the world. One of the earlier groups that Iran planted and supported was Hizbollah. This was a Shiite group in Lebanon whose mission was to overturn the government there and establish an Islamic nation. Lebanon was a country that was led by the Christian majority.

Iran also supported the establishment of the Islamic nation in Sudan. Hasan al-Turabi, the leader of *Al-Jepha Al-Islamia*, overturned the Sudanese government and established an Islamic nation there. Iran's support of Islamic movements traveled across many countries, including Egypt, Algeria, Tunisia, and many other Arab countries.

IRAQ STRIKES IRAN

Fear and terror struck the Arab countries of the Gulf. They were threatened by the Iranian project of exporting revolution into their countries. Saddam Hussein, the ruler of Iraq, had no intention of sharing his authority with fundamentalist Muslims or anyone else. He led the regional defense against the Iranian revolution and invaded Iran. All the Arab countries and the rest of the world supported him.

The Iraqi military invaded 30 percent of the Iranian homeland. The Iranians took advantage of this opportunity to defend their home and become martyrs in the name of Allah. It took two years of war for the Iranians to kick the Iraqi military out of their land. The Iranians did not stop at the border. They took the war into Iraqi soil for six more years.

The Iran/Iraq war killed almost one million Muslims from both sides, and two million were wounded. This war was intended to slow down Iran's project of exporting their movement to the Arab countries. However, the mission became stronger, and the project of spreading Islam to the world never stopped.

The Iranian revolution sent a new hope to all Islamic movements in the world. That new hope was that Islam would take over the earth and lead the world.

Chapter 18

TREACHERY BETWEEN TERRORISTS

Egypt's Militant Fundamentalists Nearly Self-Destruct

I N 1980 A situation was developing in Egypt that would cause a great setback to those pursuing jihad. The Egyptian leaders of the Islamic Group Movement (IGM) felt that they should get out of the spiritual and mental preparation time and make the move to overturn the Egyptian government. They also believed it was time to join with Sudan and Iran (who had already established Islamic states) and get the invasion of the Arab world completed so that they could move on to the worldwide vision.

The IGM divided Egypt into regions and assigned strong leaders to each region. Those regions and their leaders were:

- Al-Minya region: Karim Zohdi, Fouad Al-Dolabi, Assim Abdul-Majed, Ayman al-Zawahiri (later he became the right-hand man of Osama bin Laden), and Essam Dirbala

- Asyut region: Najeh Ibrahim and Osama Hafez

- Sohaj region: Hamdi Abdul Rahman

- Nagh Hamadi region: Ali Sharif and Talat Qusam

All these regional leaders were led by General Prince Halmmi Al-Gazar and his assistant, Essam Al-Aryan.[1]

A Move to Join the Two Groups

This newly organized Islamic Group Movement was a threat to the leadership of the Muslim Brotherhood. Omar Al-Talmasani, the leader of the Muslim Brotherhood Movement, also disagreed with the timing of their plans. He told all Muslims, "It is not the right time for jihad yet." He advised the leaders of IGM to learn some patience, not hastiness.

He also declared it was not good for the unity of Muslims to have two different movements. He suggested that they should unite under his leadership so they could be more effective.

The leader of IGM, his assistant, and the Al-Minya region leaders immediately welcomed the call for unity, claiming the Quranic verse, "Verily, Allah loves those who fight in His Cause in rows (ranks) as if they were a solid structure" (Surah 61:4, *The Noble Quran*). He said this verse spoke of the unity that Muslims should have.

The IGM leadership invited the leader of the Muslim Brotherhood to go to the southern region of Egypt to have the ceremony of unity. However, many other members of the IGM disagreed with the call for unity. As soon as the delegation from the Muslim Brotherhood arrived, a storm of rage swept through the IGM members. Those who rejected the idea of unity attempted to attack the leader of the Muslim Brotherhood. The members who were for unity defended him by killing the fellow members who disagreed.

TERRORIZING FELLOW MUSLIMS

What followed was a war between civilians fought with knives and swords. The Egyptian citizens who lived in the regions of Asyut and Al Minya lived in terror of this conflict. Members of the group who opposed unity went to their fellow members' homes and knocked on the doors. When the doors were opened, they stabbed the people of the house to death. Before the victim breathed his last breath, he was told he was a betrayer of Allah and Islam; therefore, he was receiving the punishment of whoever delayed jihad as stated by the Quran.

Many times the IGM members of the house were not home, but this did not stop the attackers. They slaughtered the wives and children, telling them the same message. Hundreds of members took trains from all over the country and came to this troubled region to stop the rage and save their movement.

Through bloodshed and terror, IGM members who opposed unity took over. They submitted the remainder of both movements to their authority. This bloody storm almost wiped out the IGM.

AL-JIHAD IS BORN

Out of IGM, the Muslim Brotherhood, and other smaller groups, a new splinter group called *al-Jihad*, emerged. It was led by Mohammed Abdul-Salam Farag. In the mid-1980s they accomplished a number of murders, including the murders of philosophers, journalists, and the head of the Egyptian Parliament.

Egyptian al-Jihad leaders appearing in court: (from left) Tarek al-Zomor
(twenty-five-year sentence) and Abod al-Zomor (forty-year sentence).

Al-Jihad in Egypt was greatly advanced by a chance
meeting that occurred when Farag visited the home of one
of the movement's members, Tarek Al-Zomor. At the time
Zomor was also hosting his brother-in-law, who was a
high-ranking Egyptian military intelligence officer (Abod
Al-Zomor).

Egyptian al-Jihad leaders appear in court: (from left) Assim Abdul-Majed
(forty-year sentence), Abod al-Zomor (forty-year sentence), Karim Zohdi (forty-
year sentence) and Hamdi Abdul Rahman (fifteen-year sentence).

There was a real bonding among these three men. They vowed to each other to do whatever it would take to overturn the Egyptian government and liberate Egypt from apostate and infidel leadership.

This took place in the summer of 1980. Abod Al-Zomor said, "I wished many times to step out from under the government's authority and start fighting the government. Now, after meeting Farag, we got like-minded to organize the right plan to establish the goal of the Islamic government."

Soon after that historical meeting took place, the leaders of al-Jihad (Abod Al-Zomor, Karim Zohdi, Fouad Al-Dolabi, and Nabil Al-Magrabi) met to organize the movement and set up an operating system. After long discussions they decided to have a committee of counselors.[2]

The committee agreed to focus on appointing, managing, and making the necessary decisions. They also agreed to spin off from the committee three minor committees:

- Preparation committee—its responsibility was to organize and prepare weapons and transportation.

- Economic committee—its responsibility was to raise the necessary finances to accomplish the mission.

- Distribution and awareness committee—it was in charge of preparing and distributing literature to those involved in upcoming jihad.

The committee of counselors divided the country into regions and set up the committee members as princes over these regions.[3]

The committee gave the right to all leaders to choose their

own assistants for these regions. Each region was responsible for its own military training and funding. Now the movement of al-Jihad was truly a reality in Egypt. Later it would reproduce itself throughout the rest of the Islamic world.

The most well-known offspring is al-Jihad in Palestine. Its leaders were trained by Egyptian radicals, and you can see similarities in their methods. For example, al-Jihad in Egypt had two men strap bombs to their bodies and blow themselves up in an attempt to kill the Egyptian minister of national security. In the same way al-Jihad in Palestine sends people on suicide missions

THE PHILOSOPHY OF AL-JIHAD

Al-Jihad was organized. Now it needed a strong philosophy to bind its members together. This philosophy was found in a book called *The Missing Commitments (Al-Fareda Al-Gaaba)* written by an engineer named Mohammed Abed al-Salem.

The author of this book met with the southern Egypt region's leader (Karim Zohdi), who made the book the by-laws of al-Jihad.

I would like to summarize the book, which is written in three chapters. The book emphasizes jihad as the only way for Islam to rise again. However, the author takes his book one step further than any other book by saying, "The Islamic invasion is coming to Rome." Previous Muslim writers had focused on the Arab world and some of the African countries; however, in this book al-Salem started talking about invading Europe and the West. Here are samples of al-Salem's opinions:

Compromised Muslims are condemned.

Fundamentalist Islamic authority must be established in every nation—it doesn't make any difference whether Muslims like it or not. It is the command of Allah, and it must be done. Al-Salem said the crucial question to answer is this: "Are we living in a true Islamic nation?"

He questioned the leadership of many Muslim countries: "How can they be sincere Muslims? They were raised and influenced in Judaism, Christianity and Communism." He felt these leaders were Muslims by name only. He declared them all to be apostates, infidels, and heathens who should be killed.

He also emphasized that the punishment should be harder on these Muslims than on the heathens. He agreed with fourteenth-century scholar Ibn Taymiyah and wrote, "Muslims should not mix with anyone else, and if they do, they should be killed as well."

Jihad supersedes other duties.

He condemned all other religious activities in Islam, such as fasting, prayer, and charitable works because they keep Muslims so busy that they ignore the call of jihad.

Killing is the Muslim's responsibility.

Killing is the big difference between Islam and all other religions. Ahed Al-Salem wrote that before Islam, Allah dealt with infidels and heathens sometimes with fires, sometimes with floods, and sometimes with other ways. However, since the establishment of Islam, Allah commanded Muslims to take the law into their own hands; it became their responsibility to torture and kill the enemies of Allah.

Jihad is offensive, not defensive.

Abed al-Salem attacked the Muslims who believed that jihad was just to defend Islam. He aggressively emphasized that jihad is not negotiable—nor can it be compromised. Jihad is the call to all Muslims. To support his point of view, he gave examples of the prophet Muhammad's letters to the kings of countries, of how the early Muslims fought, and of how Islam spread by the sword. He said that Islam should be spread this way today.

The enemy is redefined.

He also defined the enemies in a new way. They were:

- Heathens

- Muslims not governed according to Allah's law and the Quran

Abed al-Salem supported fighting those Muslims who did not live according to his interpretation of Islam.

War strategies are set in place.

Al-Salem allotted a large portion of his book to the Islamic methods of war and jihad: attacks, murders, deceit, perfidy, foul play, treachery, and breach of faith. He also explained how women, children, and all other material possessions of the enemy belong to the Muslims and their military; Muslims should exterminate anyone who fights back.

THE NEXT STEP

Al-Jihad had its foundation in place. Its hope was to follow the path of Iran and create the next truly Islamic state. Al-Jihad needed to raise funds, and its members decided to copy Muhammad's methods. In the next chapter you will learn what they did.

Chapter 19

AL-JIHAD PREPARES AND ATTACKS

Christian Businesses Robbed to Raise Funds

A S AL-JIHAD PREPARED for war in the 1980s, they needed guns, bombs, weapons, and transportation. They found themselves under tremendous pressure to come up with large sums of money. The Muslims were not committed enough to give this amount of support.

According to the Egyptian court records, an investigation found that the movement received a personal donation from Abod Al-Zomor of four thousand Egyptian pounds, several automatic machine guns, six tear-gas bombs, four RBG bombs, seven Russian bombs, Russian Kalashnikov guns, and several hand guns. These were donated from his personal cache. But these donations and many others were not enough to support the movement. They had to find another source of support.

TERRORIZING THE CHRISTIAN MINORITY

A criminal Islamic solution was presented by Ali Sharif, the leader of Quna and Nagh Hamadi regions. He suggested that the movement should take the possessions of the Egyptian Christian minority (15–17 percent of the population) and use them for support. His idea was nothing new. The el Kharij movement of the seventh century had the same philosophy: "Their women and all possessions are our rights." The idea went all the way back to Muhammad killing his enemies and plundering their cities.

This hellish idea created not a question of morality but of execution—how? How can we get the Christians' possessions? Should we rob them, enforce the *jizyah* (special taxation for unbelievers), or use extortion? Should we target the possessions of the Christian citizens only or of the churches also?

The Christian citizenry dominated several different industries in Egypt, one of these being the production of gemstones and jewelry. The idea was to attack the businesses, kill the Christians, and confiscate all money and merchandise.

After the committee heard this idea, there was a long silence. The Asyut region leader, Najeh Ibrahim, broke the silence by saying, "This is nothing but a heavenly inspiration."

Then the Al Minya region leader, Karim Zohdi, added, "We should start with any business that supports the churches and their ministry." The committee agreed, and Ali Sharif became responsible to plan the first attack.

From the records of the court's sessions we can hear the testimony from one man who witnessed an attack:

> On July 26, 1981 at noon I was in the jewelry store of Nabi Masud Askaros, in the city of Nagh Hamadi. The owner, his workers and a few customers were in the store. I heard several shots at the door of the store. I immediately hid under a table. I saw two men carrying automatic machine guns. They were wearing facemasks and gloves. They fired at the owner and also at Zarif Shinooda. They took all of the merchandise and money and, while fleeing, continued firing their guns. In the meantime, I found

out that they did the same thing to Fouad and his brother, Fah'iz, Masud's jewelry store. Six men were killed and two were injured in that store. The two robbers got in a Peugot and took off.

The Christian community lived in great terror during this time because many were killed, and they wondered who would be next.

The court record indicates that the movement got a lot of support from Egyptian Muslims who worked in oil-producing countries. The donations that were discovered included 21,000 in dollars, 10,400 in German marks, 26,000 in Egyptian pounds, and much more. All of this wasn't enough money, so they started stealing vehicles belonging to Christian church personnel. These vehicles were then transported to the desert, disassembled, and sold as used parts so that the police would not be able to track them down.

Al-Jihad killed, robbed, and stole from Christians as they were taught by the Quran regarding the People of the Book—Jews and Christians.

> Fight against…those who acknowledge not the religion of truth (i.e. Islam) among the people of the Scripture (Jews and Christians), until they pay the *Jizyah* [tax] with willing submission, and feel themselves subdued.
> —SURAH 9:29, THE NOBLE QURAN

The application of this verse would have been difficult in Egypt because of the large Christian population—there were too many Christians to kill them all. However, this was still the movement's goal—to apply the Islamic law and force Christians to pay a high taxation to Muslims, or they would be killed.

Now al-Jihad was ready and able to go in for the first major confrontation with the Egyptian government and its system. They planned to overturn the system and submit Egypt to be the base of the worldwide Islamic nations' revolution.

During this time the committee of counselors added eleven new members, but they felt that they needed one man to lead them through this major historical operation. After much thinking they decided to elect Sheikh Omar Abdel Rahman, the professor of Quranic science that I sat under at Al-Azhar University. Though blind, he was more than capable of leading such a movement.

PRESIDENT SADAT ASSASSINATED

Sheikh Abdel Rahman issued a *fatwa* that President Sadat and his government were apostate infidels who all must die. The plan to overturn the country included these steps:

1. Kill the president.

2. Gain control over strategic places in Cairo, such as the defense department, national security department, and the national radio and TV stations.

3. Take over the Asyut region in South Egypt and call the Muslim Egyptians to come out for a new Islamic revolution.

For their sharpshooter, al-Jihad commissioned Khaled al-Islambouli, who was a soldier in the Egyptian military and the national champion in long-range shooting. He was also an active member of al-Jihad.

Everything started out according to plan. On October 6, 1981, the president was shot and killed during an annual military celebration of winning the 1973 Israeli war. The Asyut region was in the hands of the movement, but they did not succeed in taking over Cairo.

After the assassination of Sadat, Vice President Mubarak immediately ordered the military to go and liberate the Asyut region from the movement's control. The government was able to arrest the leadership of al-Jihad, including Sheikh Omar Abdel Rahman. They all stood before Egypt's highest military court.

The question now was, how could the legal system in an Arabic, supposedly Islamic, country deal with these Muslims who obeyed the call of Islam according to the Quran? Let's look at the court record of perhaps the most crucial case in Egyptian history.

Chapter 20

JUSTICE LOSES, QURAN WINS

Sheikh Uses Quran to Defend Assassination and Win Release

T WAS SHEIKH Omar Abdel Rahman's moment to show his talents to the court.

He stood before the court to defend the philosophy of the al-Jihad movement. He had the floor twice—once to explain to the jury the mind-set of jihad, and once to respond to the questions of the attorney general. When you read carefully the court transcript and his answers, you will see Islam's true colors. Sheikh Abdel Rahman, the scholar of the Quran and Islamic law, put his expertise to work for the movement in a way that no one ever expected.

He led the attorney general to play the game that he mastered all of his life. He succeeded in turning the table of accusation and putting the attorney general on the defense. Sheikh Omar Abdel Rahman set the stage for himself in the

(Courtesy of Sinai Publishing, Cairo, Egypt)

Sheikh Omar Abdel Rahman appearing before the Egyptian Supreme Court after the assassination of President Anwar Sadat.

first round. He made the following Islamic principles clear to the court:

- Justice should be according to what Allah has set for the Muslims only. Allah's lordship should be acknowledged by all Muslims, and no one can deny it because Allah created everything and everyone. He has the absolute right to his creation.

- The people who carry out Islamic justice should be faithful believers who obey Allah's commands and the prophet Muhammad's teaching. If the justice system is not run according to the Quran, Muslim believers should not submit themselves to its laws.

- The imported laws from infidel countries, "USA and Europe," are man-made and not according to Allah's laws. The existing law of Egypt is influenced by men who compromise Allah's law in many areas such as adultery, gambling, homosexuality, alcoholism, and theft. Anyone who modifies Allah's laws is an apostate infidel. Anyone who submits to these laws is also an apostate infidel.

Sheikh Abdel Rahman established the authority of his words by claiming, "What I'm saying is not opinion or one person's spiritual ideas, but it is what Allah's book says."

Following is a portion of the court transcript during the final court session, when the attorney general questioned the sheikh.[1]

Attorney General: In Islamic history we find many Muslims who claimed that Allah is the ultimate judge but acted any way they pleased. Islam called them *el-Kharij*. Islamic society rejects them.

Sheikh Rahman: *Kharij* are those who rebelled against or disobeyed the Islamic successor, so who is the Islamic successor today? Where is Ali ibn Abi Talib today? And if you call us *Kharij*, it means that we disobeyed or rebelled from the successor, the Muslim leader. So who is today's successor and leader of Muslims? Is he the friend of Jews, the supporter of Israel and Begin's buddy? [He referred to peace talks between President Sadat, Menachem Begin, prime minister of Israel, and Jimmy Carter, US president. Sadat was the recipient of the Nobel Peace Prize at this time.] Is our successor the man who abandoned Allah's law and commanded compliance with the laws of heathens and infidels?

Attorney General· The belief that Allah is the lawmaker and the only judge does not mean that if our Islamic society finds solutions according to our social and mental standards of living today that so doing makes it an apostate, infidel society.

Sheikh Rahman: Disobeying Allah and his law in the name of convenience has only

155

one meaning—these are sinful, lost infidels who have made their own laws and abandoned Allah's laws. They are the ones whom Allah commanded the Muslims to kill in jihad.

Attorney General: Jihad is not killing. This is not Islam's teaching. Jihad is a spiritual fight against evil, poverty, sickness, and sin. Killing is only from the devil.

Sheikh Rahman: From where does the attorney general come up with this understanding? Are there verses in the Quran that I don't know about that say jihad is a spiritual fight against evil, poverty, sickness, and sin? Perhaps there is new inspiration from Allah that our attorney general received recently and the rest of the Muslims do not yet know.

Attorney General: Declaring that our Islamic society is heathen, infidels, or apostates is an insult on our merciful Allah, his commands, and his law.

Sheikh Rahman: Which commands and laws are you talking about? The ones that compromised adultery, gambling, and alcohol? Is this not our merciful Allah's command? Mr. Attorney General, your commands and laws are from the devil.

Attorney General: If any Muslim society confesses that Allah is the only God and

Muhammad is his prophet, no one has the right to accuse them of being infidels.

Sheikh Rahman: What you say is not the real truth. Someone can confess that Allah is God and Muhammad is his prophet, but he can do something against his confession, and this takes him outside of Islam.

Attorney General: President Al-Sadat was a great man who sacrificed his life for the love of Allah and the love of his country.

Sheikh Rahman: Do you know how this man sacrificed his life for the love of his country? He is the same man who declared that all religions are equal. He made the infidels and the grandchildren of "monkeys and pigs" [*monkeys* and *pigs* is the description the Quran uses for the Jewish people] equal to the Muslims. He made the world's greatest criminal murderer his dear friend [referring to Begin, Israel's prime minister]. The same man who sacrificed his life for Allah broke all of Allah's laws in this country. The same man who worshiped Allah sarcastically described the Muslim women's veil as a tent. This man loved Allah? He also insulted Allah when he danced with and hugged women publicly before the international media and before the whole world. [In celebration of the peace agreement, Sadat and his wife danced with Carter and his wife on national television.] This contradicts what Sadat always preached about village behavior. This man led our country to free enterprise and nearly destroyed our economy. He led our country to a moral and social disaster, and it will take our country many years to recover from him.

You have witnessed, dear reader, how Sheikh Omar Abdel Rahman not only defeated the attorney general, but how he also defeated the justice system in Egypt.

Yes, jihad means killing all the enemies of Allah and Islam. Yes, Muslims believe in taking the law into their own hands and killing Allah's enemies, as if he can't handle them himself. Yes, the laws of the land could not overrule the Quran. Yes, the mastermind of the murder of the president could justify his acts through the Quran and be declared not guilty in the highest court of a great nation, Egypt. What a shame.

Sheikh Abdel Rahman was set free officially because they did not have material evidence that he was the one who gave al-Jihad the religious order to kill Sadat as an infidel. In my opinion the blind sheikh's own words were more than enough evidence for a conviction.

However, the crime did not go unpunished. Five men were executed military style, including Khaled al-Islambouli, the sharpshooter, and Mohammed Abed al-Salem, the author of *The Missing Commitments*. When the police arrested the author, they confiscated all his books and burned them. It can only be found on the black market now.

In spite of the tremendous resistance of the Egyptian government, al-Jihad survived, grew, and never stopped. Many of the leaders of the al-Jihad movement were able to flee to other countries, such as Sudan, Yemen, Pakistan, and Czechoslovakia. A large number went to Afghanistan to become a part of the al-Jihad movement there.

Later they united with Osama bin Laden, who based his movement on the same beliefs and principles. Those leaders who fled from Egypt, the original members of al-Jihad, helped bin Laden to establish a new movement. They named it al Qaeda. Dr. Ayman al-Zawahiri, one of the Egyptian al-Jihad leaders, became bin Laden's right hand man and later the leader of al Qaeda. Afghanistan became the place of refuge for those who were persecuted by the Egyptian government.

Later the fundamentalist Islamic group in Afghanistan, the Taliban, welcomed all these men and supported them as partners in the same call of jihad—ready to be partners in death but hoping to be the victors when Allah's people rule the world.

(Courtesy of Sinai Publishing, Cairo, Egypt)

Khaled al-Islambouli, put to death by the Egyptian government in 1982 as the sharpshooter who assassinated President Anwar Sadat.

Chapter 21

JIHAD BLEEDS OUT OF EGYPT

Egyptian Leaders Travel to Surrounding Countries

WHEN YOU THROW a stone into the water, the ripples go in all directions. This is what happens with militant fundamentalist groups. A major event in one country causes a ripple effect in many other countries.

Egypt is like the stone that was tossed into the water. It is at the center of modern terrorism. The reason for this is that Egypt is the capital of Islamic education for the entire world. Al-Azhar University sends missionaries everywhere to spread Islam.

If there are religious questions in a Muslim nation anywhere in the world, they ask Al-Azhar. When I was in South Africa, if the Muslims had a question they couldn't answer, they wrote to Al-Azhar. For example, they needed a ruling on when to start Ramadan, which depends on the sighting of the new moon. Al-Azhar declared that when they could see the moon in Cairo, the world could start Ramadan.

At the time when Muslim Brotherhood, IGM, al-Jihad, and others were developing, I was immersed in Al-Azhar University. I spent eleven years there, earning my bachelor's, master's, and doctorate degrees. In addition, after I earned my bachelor's degree, the university sent me out as a visiting professor to Islamic universities in other countries, including Tunisia, Libya, Iraq, and Morocco. From this vantage point, I observed what was happening.

We've looked in detail at the uprisings in Egypt and

Iran. Now let's see the ripple effects of Sadat's assassination in North Africa. Going west from Egypt, the movement traveled to Libya, Tunisia, and Algeria. Going south, effects were felt in Sudan.

LIBYA

Next door to Egypt thousands of Libyan Muslim men were inspired by the murder of Sadat. They too were willing to die in the name of Allah and for the cause of jihad.

The Libyan Muslims organized many movements to assassinate Muammar Qaddafi and overturn his government. After a brief civil war Qaddafi was finally deposed and killed on October 20, 2011.

Though Qaddafi was a Muslim, many Westerners may not recognize that his position was far from Islamic fundamentalism. After he took over in 1969, he ruled the country with a constitution not Islamic law. His original goal was to create a democracy.

Qaddafi admired the past president of Egypt, Gamal Abdel Nasser, for his harsh methods in dealing with the Muslim Brotherhood Movement. (President Nasser was well known for his zero tolerance of radicals. Twice he gathered them and slaughtered them—in 1954 and 1965.) Qaddafi took every opportunity to call radical Muslims "the street dogs" on Libyan national television. He followed Nasser's methods: he slaughtered radicals many times to eliminate their influence in his country.

The Libyan members of these Islamic radical groups fought against Qaddafi for two main reasons: 1) his anti-Islamic political ideology and 2) his dictatorship and corruption.

Eventually during the Arab Spring, with the support of

the Western countries (especially France and the United States), they were able to put an end to his regime and capture Qaddafi and kill him publicly.

The vast majority of the Libyan people stood behind these groups during the Libyan revolution. They were hoping that after getting rid of Qaddafi and his regime that these groups would be united and bring a new beginning, forming an Islamic government and leading Libya into justice, freedom, and prosperity.

After the elimination of Qaddafi, however, people witnessed nothing in their country but division, chaos, violence, killing, and destruction. This caused quite a good percentage of the Libyan people to wish they had not gotten rid of Qaddafi's regime. This situation reflects the real dilemma not just in Libya but also in many other countries of the Middle East, such as Egypt, Yemen, Iraq, and Syria.

TUNISIA

The influence of the Egyptian al-Jihad traveled from Libya into Tunisia. Among the participants were Rashid al-Ghannoushi, the exiled leader and articulate spokesman of al-Nahda, Tunisia's Islamic opposition movement. They were in constant struggle with the previous president Habib ibn Ali Bourguiba and president Zine El Abidine Ben Ali.

I visited Tunisia in the early 1990s, and the Muslims treated me with great respect because I came from the country of Islamic heroes. They called Khaled al-Islambouli a modern Islamic hero for killing Sadat. They told me, "Our Islamic Arab nations need people like that to overturn all of the infidels' governments and establish the Islamic dynasty just as in Muhammad's days."

ALGERIA

To fully appreciate the effect in Algeria, we need to look at the unique history of this country. It was one of the first areas to be conquered by Islam.

Within ten years of the death of Muhammad, the Islamic military invaded Algeria. From that point on Algeria remained an Islamic state under the Islamic empire until the French invaded it in 1830. The French occupied Algeria until 1962. The French influence was so strong in the Algerian culture that even after the liberation, French remained the main language; throughout most of the country the Arabic language was almost forgotten.

After the Algerian revolution that was led by Ahmed Ben Bella, Algeria was governed by a national government that was not Islamic based. Many Arab Muslim countries helped Algeria to overcome the French influence and establish Islam and the Arabic language. My uncle was one of the head missionaries sent by Al-Azhar University to Algeria to teach the Arabic language and to reinstall Islam.

Slowly but surely Algeria became an Arabic country again. In the process Algeria was influenced by two major Egyptian organizations: Al-Azhar University's educational mission and the Muslim Brotherhood Organization.

During Egyptian president Nasser's tremendous persecution of the Muslim Brotherhood Organization between 1954 and 1960, many of its members immigrated to Algeria. They spread their beliefs among the new generation of Algerians.

Ali Belhadj and Dr. Abbas al-Madani, who were

professors at the University of Algiers, started a new Islamic movement called *al-Gabha al-Aslamia Lilncaz,* meaning Islamic Salvation Front. This was just a new name for the Muslim Brotherhood of Egypt. This movement had a strong relationship with other Islamic movements across the Arab countries, especially Egypt.

The leaders of the Algerian and the Egyptian movements worked closely together to lead all Islamic movements in the world at the time. These two groups worked hard to enter Morocco, Tunisia, and Libya to establish the Islamic nation across North Africa. They planned to unite with the movements in Sudan and Iran so that the world would see the reestablishment of the Islamic authority throughout the Arabic region.

Muammar Qaddafi immediately felt a threat to his government in Libya. He was pressured from the east by the Egyptians and from the west by the Algerians. Qaddafi volunteered to help the existing government of Algeria fight the radical groups and their leaders, al-Madani and Belhadj.

Hijacking an election

In the early nineties the leaders of the Islamic Salvation Front hosted one of history's largest rallies for Islamic fundamentalist groups. They jam-packed the national soccer stadium. The Algerian capital will always remember the crowd's cheers that day: "Allah is great! Patience, patience, all ye Jews! Muhammad's forces are on the way."

All these anti-Jewish hate cheers were inspired by the guest speaker, Khaled al-Islambouli's mother. Yes, the mother of President Sadat's assassin, who was put to death by the Egyptian government, spoke to the leaders of jihad in Algeria.

During her speech she inspired the crowd to sacrifice their money as well as their souls to make jihad a reality in their country and the world. She stated that she gave one son as a sacrifice for jihad, and she was willing to present her other son, Mohammed, who was standing on stage beside her, to the same cause—to see the banner of Islam take over the world. She said that she was willing to die herself to bring victory to Islam over the enemy.

The crowds cheered aggressively when she said, "Nothing made me more proud as a mother than that my son Khaled was sentenced to death by the enemy of Islam." She ignited the spirit of jihad and martyrdom in everyone's heart when they heard her saying how many roads and streets were already named in honor of her son in Islamic nations around the world. She added, "Even the enemies of Islam look at my son as a hero for giving his life for what he believes in." She quoted one of the prophet Muhammad's teachings in hadith, "Any nation that abandons jihad will be conquered and subdued."[1]

Make no mistake; this woman left the crowd in the flames of hate toward their government. She prepared the Algerian movement for what would happen in their battle to overturn the government. The impact of this rally was electrifying. It gave the Muslims in Algeria the courage to carry out their mission.

Not long after this rally a new election was held (1991). The Islamic Salvation Front used this opportunity to manipulate the election for their personal gain, hoping to take over. The movement won the election by scaring all other candidates out of running for office; however, it was not going to take over the country that easily.

The Algerian upper class, the elites, and the highly educated citizens immediately rose up to warn and object to the existing government turning over authority to these radicals. Many of the Arabic countries such as Egypt, Libya, Tunisia, and Morocco were familiar with the danger of these groups. They also warned the government about the results of letting the radicals take over. Algeria had no other option but to order the military to secure the country and cancel the election. This was the beginning of the long battle between the military and the Islamic movement that continues to this day.

In the 1990s more than one hundred fifty thousand people were killed to keep fundamentalist Islam from ruling their nation. The Algerian government arrested the leaders of the Islamic Salvation Front, but it could not stop the bloodshed. Afghanistan sent in many experienced fighters to try to unseat the government.

And the bloody struggle continues.

SUDAN

Sheikh Omar Abdel Rahman went south to Sudan after he was released from prison. He spent a few months there with Dr. Hasan al-Turabi, the leader of the Sudanese movement *al-Islamia*. Al-Turabi had succeeded in overturning the Sudanese government and taking over the country with the help of one of the generals of the Sudanese military.

Al-Turabi's movement was established except for the Christian minority in south Sudan. However, al-Turabi is getting rid of them. Al-Turabi has slaughtered Christians, cutting off their hands and legs, injecting them with the HIV virus—just as Islam taught him. He has shown the world what Islam will do to Christians if it can.

The Sudanese Christians refuse to convert to Islam. They are also poor and cannot afford to pay for the high taxation of being Christians; therefore, they are dying by the thousands under the authority of al-Turabi. Al-Turabi's Islamic authority has killed Christian men, gathered Christian women and children, and sold them into slavery. Many humanitarian organizations have rushed in to buy these Christian slaves and set them free.

SUMMARY

In summary, though the highly organized fundamentalist group in Egypt did not succeed in overturning its own government, the people who were a part of it went out to influence radical groups in other countries, particularly Libya, Tunisia, Algeria, and Sudan.

These movements are gradually becoming a part of our world, and their mission is to take over. They're always waiting for the right environment or a conflict to happen.

Chapter 22

NEW STRATEGY: ATTACK THE WEST

Sheikh Omar Abdel Rahman and Osama bin Laden

THE PRACTICE OF terrorism has evolved since the early seventies in two points—first, the target and second, the method. In the early seventies we started to see a major shift in the targets of terrorism. Terrorists used to target certain individuals such as diplomatic figures, high-ranking military officials, and politicians. Today terrorism is no longer threatening individuals, but instead it is focused on the general public.

Random attacks on the public are more effective because they terrorize the majority and spread fear in a larger way. They give terrorists fast results and more bargaining power to get what they want. Terrorism has become a method of political debate and dialogue.

SHEIKH OMAR ABDEL RAHMAN COMES TO AMERICA

After Sheikh Abdel Rahman won his case in front of the Egyptian supreme court, he was given his freedom. He went to Sudan and was welcomed by his fellow jihad leader Dr. Hasan al Turabi. Sheikh Abdel Rahman spent a few months there, giving him support.

Then Sheikh Abdel Rahman decided to make a new move toward bringing back the glory of Islam. This time the goal was not to fight any one country—he was pursuing global jihad. Remember, Sayyid Qutb and other writers emphasized the importance of taking jihad to the world and establishing a worldwide Islamic nation.

Sheikh Abdel Rahman was now after what Muslims call the source of infidelity and evil—America and Europe. To work toward this goal, Sheikh Abdel Rahman decided to take advantage of the freedom and democracy that exist only in the West. He came to America.

When Sheikh Abdel Rahman arrived in New Jersey, he received a great welcome from the Muslim leaders of the United States. He settled in New Jersey and immediately started meetings at al-Salaam Mosque in Jersey City. Muslims from all over the United States also invited him to come and teach them. He held seminars and training sessions in many major cities.

What do you think he was teaching them? Love, peace, and forgiveness in Islam? Not at all! He taught the American Muslims the true meaning of jihad. He called all American Muslims to unite and work together for the call of Islam, the call for Islam to once again rule the world.

1993 World Trade Center Attack

The only goal of Sheikh Abdel Rahman's residency in the United States was to lead jihad from within. The following are his objectives:

- To base the Islamic jihad movement in nations of the infidels—these are his own words—in preparation for the worldwide revolution

- To pressure the US government by threatening America's security from within

- To use this pressure to change US policies
  in the Islamic world—particularly to break
  down support for Israel and to resolve the
  Palestinian dilemma

America supports Israel and different governments in the Middle East that are considered secular by Muslim fundamentalists. Sheikh Abdel Rahman believes these governments should all be overturned by the sword of Islam. Therefore, America's support for them makes it the world's greatest obstacle to the Islamic jihad movement.

Sheikh Abdel Rahman's first operation of business was to shake the United States by attacking one of the foremost symbols of prosperity, success, and free enterprise— the towers of the World Trade Center in New York City. In 1993, as the world heard, the jihad movement was responsible for a major explosion in one of the towers, killing six people. For leading this attack, Sheikh Abdel Rahman will be in a US federal prison for life. Yes, he's still alive, and we are feeding and providing for him with taxpayers' money while he continues to inspire the jihad movement from behind bars.

OBSTACLES TO WORLDWIDE REVOLUTION

The Islamic movement believes there are three main ideologies that stand in the way of worldwide Islamic revolution.

1. Judaism, as manifested in Israel

2. Christianity, as manifested in the United States and the West

3. Communism, as manifested in the former Soviet Union and China

They also believe these obstacles must be destroyed before the revolution will take place.

AMERICA AS A SPECIAL TARGET

There are five clear reasons why America is a special target of Islamic fundamentalists:

1. America represents those whom the Quran calls "People of the Book"—Jews and Christians.

2. America supports Israel.

3. America is the source of all that Muslims consider to be evil—pornography, alcohol, homosexual rights, evil music, evil fashion, and evil culture.

4. America supports Christianity all over the world. More Christian missionaries come from the United States than any other country.

5. America is a government "of the people, by the people, and for the people," which makes it a heathen government in Muslim thinking because Allah is to be the head of all government.

America and the West are seen as the true enemies of Allah and Islam. The West is always helping Arab governments to kill the Muslim fundamentalists and destroy their organizations. Also, the West helps Israel fight and kill the Arabs.

OSAMA BIN LADEN

There was a new leader in the Islamic movement. He was a Saudi millionaire with a history similar to Sheikh Abdel Rahman's. He left his home country because of persecution from the government and went to Sudan for a short time, just as Abdel Rahman did. In 1996 he left to go to Afghanistan to unite with Dr. Ayman al-Zawahiri and other original members of the Egyptian al-Jihad to establish the al Qaeda organization. This is an international organization that includes non-Arab members such as Chechnya, Kashmir, Uzbekistan, Pakistan, Kenya, and many others. The people are different, but the goal is the same: to declare war on the West, the United States, and Israel. Israel is condemned for representing Judaism, and the United States is condemned for representing Christianity. He was killed by US forces on May 2, 2011.

THE AL QAEDA ORGANIZATION

Osama bin Laden did not start from nothing. Al Qaeda is a repackaging, regrouping, and reorganization of the Egyptian al-Jihad experience. However, al Qaeda is different in the following three areas:

Mind-set: attacking Western targets

Previous Islamic movements believed that they should start locally—overturn their homeland first, establish a nation that is solely based on Islamic authority, and then overtake the world. After their failure to take control of Egypt in the eighties, Dr. Zawahiri and Sheikh Abdel Rahman concluded that it would be better to go for worldwide jihad. They decided to go after the "head" rather than the "hands."

The head was identified by its political policies. America and Europe supported Egypt to destroy the Islamic sects; America supported Iraq to fight the fundamentalists of the Iranian revolution; and America is still supporting Israel to fight Palestine. Al Qaeda decided that America is the head, and the secular Arabic countries are the hands. (Remember, militant fundamentalists consider nearly all Muslim governments to be overly secular.)

Their mind-set is that if we take out the head, then the hands won't work. In other words, if we take out the big brother, then we can do whatever we want to the little brothers.

So the leadership decided the West should be the prime target for al Qaeda. Bin Laden was convinced of Sheikh Abdel Rahman's new philosophy that jihad, the battle against Islam's enemies, should be fought on the enemy's turf.

Preparation: diverse, international membership

The target is no longer the police force, the military, or the government. Now the target is civilization, economy, and the security of the world's source of power, meaning the United States and European countries. The new philosophy for the Islamic movement is one of killing civilians and destroying economies, but it's still in accordance with the Quran.

Because the target has changed, the preparation is different. Al Qaeda seeks worldwide membership, which gives the group a wide diversity of experience. Osama bin Laden was a multimillionaire, and he used all his wealth to help his movement. He also received a lot of help from the Taliban regime, which confiscated a large selection of weapons from the Russians after their war and also from the United States, which supported the Afghans' efforts against communism.

Perhaps the most important preparation for al Qaeda's members is that most of them are experienced soldiers of war. Many of bin Laden's people are survivors of the Egyptian jihad movement, the Afghanistan war, the Kashmir war, the war against Israel, and many other conflicts. These men are trained terrorists, rejected by their own governments.

Implementation: starting with smaller targets

Implementation of the plan started by learning from Sheikh Abdel Rahman's example. He failed in the first bomb attack against the World Trade Center in 1993. Al Qaeda learned from past mistakes and made better plans: they began with smaller US targets. On August 7, 1998, they bombed the US embassies in both Kenya and Tanzania, killing more than two hundred people. The US response was weak: on August 20, 1998, President Bill Clinton launched two cruise missiles against suspected terrorist sites in Sudan. Al Qaeda laughed at the Clinton administration for using multimillion-dollar missiles to blow up ten-dollar tents.

Later on October 12, 2000, al Qaeda tried to sink one of America's largest Navy ships, the *USS Cole*, as it sat in the harbor at Aden, Yemen. The bomb killed seventeen sailors, injured many others, and sent America's great ship home with a huge hole in the middle. This time the administration did not retaliate. It acted as if nothing happened. Now al Qaeda perceived a message of tolerance from the United States, and bin Laden got the green light to do bigger and worse—attacking on US soil for the first time since the 1993 bombing of the World Trade Center. On September

11, 2001, his plan was put into action as four planes were hijacked. This act resulted in the collapse of the World Trade Center and damage to the Pentagon—not to mention the deaths of everyone on board the planes.

The worldwide media was instrumental in helping al Qaeda achieve its goal of spreading fear and shaking the West's national security, especially that of the United States.

Sayyid Qutb envisioned this in his writings—Muslims moving the battleground to the infidel's homeland and ruling the world by the fear of Islam. This is what Sheikh Abdel Rahman started and Osama bin Laden continued.

Osama bin Laden learned a lot from the experience of Egyptians in al Qaeda, especially his right-hand man, Ayman al-Zawahiri, and others. You can see a lot of similarity between the technique used by the Egyptian al-Jihad in their attempt to take over the government and al Qaeda's methods against the United States. The Egyptian al-Jihad stole from Christians and used an Egyptian soldier trained by the government to use a military weapon to assassinate President Sadat. Al Qaeda stole from the United States (four aircraft) and used them to attack its targets.

The innocent Christians in cities all over Egypt (Nagh Hamadi, Abo Karacas, Al Minya, Dyroot, Malawi, Asyut, and others) were the cheap sacrifice for the Islamic terrorists' game, as were the Americans in New York and Washington, DC and the planes' passengers and flight crews.

Killing innocent people in the name of Allah is a continual practice of Islam worldwide. It is going on with millions of Christians in the south Sudan, Egypt, Nigeria, and other countries.

A good example is what happened in January 2000 in Al-Kosheh, a village in southern Egypt. Twenty-one men, women, and children were set on fire with torches and burned to death during an attack on their village. Their bodies were split open vertically from the throat down so their attackers could watch their organs pulsate; others were set on fire while still alive. The perpetrators cut opposite arms and legs off to send back to their village to spread fear.[1]

Where do militant Muslims get the ideas for their cruelty? From the Quran.

> The recompense of those who wage war against Allah and His Messenger and do mischief in the land is only that they shall be killed or crucified or their hands and their feet be cut off from opposite sides, or be exiled from the land.
> —SURAH 5:33, THE NOBLE QURAN

While this English translation says to cut off hands and feet, my understanding of the Arabic meaning is to cut off the entire arm and leg, just as they did to the Egyptian villagers.

Yes, this is happening in the twenty-first century. Of course, the Egyptian government did a good job of covering up what happened.

SECTION V

THE FUTURE OF THE MUSLIM WORLD

Chapter 23

RESPONDING TO RADICALS
IN THE MUSLIM WORLD

RADICAL ISLAMIC GROUPS are a serious threat in our world today. They are driven by Islamic teaching, motivated by the goal to live eternity in Paradise, and committed to conquer the world for Islam, and they strive for the sake of Allah until Islamic authority is the only form of government in the world.

Now you might wonder: How can we deal with this threat? What is the solution? Is there any hope for Islamic terrorism to be stopped and for peace to be established in the Middle East? Some people say we find ourselves in a "war on terrorism." I would rather call it a war of ideas.

CAN VIOLENCE STOP VIOLENCE?

Dealing with Islamic radicalism in the countries of the Muslim world is very sophisticated and difficult, and crushing out a radical group by using violence is not a solution because violence creates violence. Trying to fight radicalism by violence is like fighting a serious sickness by using a pain killer: it might stop the symptoms for the short term, but it does not bring a solution for the long term. It is better to search for the roots of the problem and to deal with it so that we can achieve a genuine and long-term solution.

The Egyptian government under President Abdul-Fattah al-Sisi decided to stop Islamic radicalism by military power, just as Nasser had done in the past. This kind of approach might work for a limited time within the national borders of a specific country. This approach, however, will never be able to fully stop the radical Islamic movements worldwide because it will not be able to erase its ideology. It will be impossible to end the strife of radical Islamists worldwide by military power.

When I witnessed the military coup in Egypt, overthrowing the democratically elected government, I was in shock. I certainly do not support Muslim Brotherhood as a group, and I do not sympathize with them in any way. But I am for a democratic process that can give everyone the chance to exercise their rights in participating in the political process of their country. Also I believe that the peaceful political approach that Muslim Brotherhood had chosen is much better than a violent one, such as practiced by ISIS or other radical groups including al Qaeda.

If someone will object my opinion, and point out that Muslim Brotherhood is a radical group who have their own agenda, my answer will be: even though I agree about that, it is better to sit around the table and to discuss these agendas in a peaceful and democratic way than to use guns, grenades, or missiles to wipe out people. It is better to let a nation hold politicians accountable through democratic elections than to go back to dictatorship.

RETHINKING FOREIGN POLICY

If we ask whether and how the problems in the Middle East can be solved from its roots, we will have to deal with the elements that have caused the conflict and keep fueling it. The first element was articulated by the young people, who went to the streets to demonstrate during the beginning of the Arab Spring, namely their hunger for bread, freedom, and social justice. A second element is the corrupt dictator regimes that the radical Muslims view as one of the first enemies of Islam because they compromise Islamic law. Western countries, who cooperate with or support these regimes are seen as equally evil.

I believe Western countries could indeed contribute to solve the situation by pursuing a fair and helpful role, sincerely seeking to help the population. So far, however, Western countries have played a quite negative role in the development of Middle Eastern countries, including Egypt. Instead of searching for a right way to promote and spread democracy in the Middle East, they often put their hand in the hand of vicious corrupt dictator regimes, seeking to secure their own interests in this region.

When the Arab Spring started with the peaceful demonstrations of the young generation, the Western countries were completely silent. They did not support or give a hand to this new generation to start a new birth of democracy and freedom in their region. Consequently the first attempt to real democracy failed. After Muslim Brotherhood and Salafist had gained influence using democratic methods, the rich corrupt Arab Gulf regimes felt severely threatened and used their oil money to put this new birth of democracy into death. They cooperated with the Egyptian military and overthrew the first freely and democratically elected government in Egyptian history. And in the neighboring countries, such as Lybia, Tunisia, and Yemen, they jeopardized the new hope for democracy by defending the old regimes and the old political systems.

It is typical for corrupt regimes to defend each other. Saudi Arabia provided a safe haven to the Tunisian dictator by giving him political asylum after he ran away from his country. United Arab Emirates provided a safe haven to the relatives and family members of the Tunisian dictator and also the Egyptian dictators (Mubarak people). And Oman provided a safe haven to the family members and the sons of the Libyan dictator Muammar Qaddafi.

The Western countries, however, including the United States ignored these facts and continued putting their hands in the hand of these corrupt regimes. This fact by itself is destroying the image of the Western countries in this region, and it is providing another reason to the upset and angry young Muslim generation who believe that the Western countries are hypocrites when they speak about democracy. Muslims complain that Western countries just seek their own interests and will partner with their oppressors and support the dictator regimes to do so.

My advice, therefore, to the United States and the rest of the Western countries is to rethink their foreign policies. They should avoid applying a double standard and show integrity instead. They should seek to help the public interest of the ordinary people, standing behind them and supporting them against their vicious dictators, instead of being a friend to the dictator regimes. The best way to secure the Western interest and to heal and strengthen the American and Western image in Muslim countries is to take the side of the people—not the side of these bad royal families. This could be a great contribution in the search for a solution to resolve the problem of radical Islam.

Chapter 24

CHALLENGING THE PHILOSOPHY BEHIND ISIS

THE TERRORISM OF Islamic radical groups such as ISIS violates the basic principles of religious, social or cultural behavior. ISIS declares itself as the only true and faithful advocate of Islam, which is taking the responsibility of enforcing Allah's will by defending Islam, the Quran, and the Prophet Muhammad. When ISIS declared through their leader Abu Bakr al-Baghdadi the restoration of the Islamic Caliphate which is known as ISIS (the Islamic state in Syria and Iraq), they used the main sources of Islamic law (the Quran and Sunnah) to justify their agenda and to legalize their behavior, including the different methods of punishment that they used against Muslims and non-Muslims.

This leads us to the crucial questions: How can we deal with this threat and what can we do to stop or prevent the spread of radical Islamic ideology? I believe the only effective way to stop this radical and violent ideology is a new interpretation of the original sources. Such a new interpretation has to be done by the scholars of Islam in order to be acceptable to Muslims. While most people, including the radical Muslims, believe that the Islamic law they hold to is perfect, divine, and unchangeable, the truth is that the Islamic law they believe and practice includes the interpretations and opinions of Islamic scholars, which cannot be considered perfect and infallible because they are just human opinions. Moreover, many violent aspects of Islamic teachings that are practiced today by radical Islamic groups such as ISIS are based on *fatwas* and interpretations that have been added by Islamic scholars and cannot be found in the Quran. They are justified by referring to hadith, which are not recognized as fully reliable. This is why many moderate or liberal Muslims call for filtering the Sunnah and for a rereading of the Quran in light of the twenty-first century.

You might wonder: But what about all the violent verses that call for jihad that *are* indeed in the Quran, which is the first primary source of Islam? The good news is that there are ways to deal even with this challenge. One of the key arguments views the call to jihad from a completely different perspective.

It can be argued that the verses concerning jihad have to be seen in the context of Islamic history. As Muhammad was targeted by aggressive enemies who tried to destroy him, he protected himself and the Islamic community through violence and aggression. Today the situation is completely different than in Muhammad's time. Islam has been established for more than fourteen hundred years and there are 1.5 billion followers of Islam worldwide. Consequently Islam has the opportunity today to peacefully coexist with others. There is no need today to convert non-Muslims or force them to follow the laws of Islam in order for the Muslim community to be safe. Therefore it can be argued that there is no longer a need for the teachings of the violent Medina-Quran and Muslims can return to the peaceful teachings of the beginning of Islam, which even speaks about religious freedom.

One basic principle that Muslims can learn from the

life example of Muhammad is that he was always very flexible to adjust to the given circumstances. As we can see from the Quran and as mentioned in this book, the rules concerning alcohol changed several times. First it was allowed. Later it was restricted, later again it was completely prohibited, and eventually Muslims were promised a river of alcohol in Paradise. There is no real consistency in the Islamic prescriptions concerning alcohol. It almost looks as if Allah changed his mind. This is just one of many examples. However, I am not saying this to make fun of Allah or the Quran. This is not my intention. The reason I am pointing out this aspect is as an example of the "flexibility" of *Sharia*. I think it is important to stress that this is not my personal opinion or discovery, but this is an aspect that Islamic scholars praise about *Sharia*: the claim that *Sharia* is flexible enough to fit with all times.

Today in the twenty-first century living circumstances are completely different from what they were during the time of Muhammad. I am fully convinced that if Muhammad were alive today, he would not live the same way he used to live in the Arabian Peninsula of his time, but this is exactly what committed Muslims usually try to do. They try to live the way Muhammad lived in his time. They wear the kind of clothing Muhammad used to wear, they eat the way Muhammad used to eat, and they try to imitate him as much as they can. Also they prefer to stick to the interpretations of the early scholars of Islam. I believe that if Muhammad were alive today, he would adjust to the current life circumstances, and I believe that Muhammad would want Muslims to reinterpret the Quran for themselves and not just to follow the (violent) interpretations of the early scholars.

Is this just my wishful thinking or is there really any

hope that this might happen, that Muslims will try to reform Islamic law? The good news is that since the establishment of ISIS more and more voices in the Arab world call for reformation. This gives me hope. And this is what I am holding to in my life and what I don't ever want to lose: faith, love, and hope.

How Should We Deal With the Threat in Our Countries?

When I witness terror attacks committed in our countries or hear in the news about the horrible acts of terror committed by ISIS, my heart is very sad. But we should not lose hope. My hope is that the shocking reports might push some moderate Muslims to rethink what kind of God they follow, and I hope it will push them to clearly distance themselves from radical Islam.

I am convinced that it will not help just complaining about the terrible things happening in our world. My personal conviction is this: "Better than cursing the darkness is to light a candle."

You might wonder what kind of candle you can light and what you can contribute to make a difference. I am convinced that it is very important to have the right attitude and that each one of us is important. How do you deal with the information you read in this book? Many people take one of two extreme positions. Some put their head in the sand and don't want to hear any of this. Others respond with fear and anger. If you feel fear or anger inside you, let me remind you that the majority of Muslims do *not* hold to the radical Islamic teachings presented in this book. Most Muslims just want to have a peaceful, good life.

My wish for our society is that the news about ISIS

attacks will cause people to rethink what kind of values they hold to and stand for. When a committed Muslim will tell you in the street that Islam has to come to the West to rescue the Western society from the moral decline, how will you respond? When Muslims see that adultery is not viewed any longer as a serious problem and that homosexuality is being legalized, they take this is as clear evidence for the moral decline of the society, and they claim the moral obligation to bring this society back to God. One of the reasons Muslims are so successful in winning young people for Islam is that many young people indeed have no more moral guidelines and deep in their hearts they feel that this is not OK. They feel that they are not OK with God. If a Muslim offers them the very easy solution to get right with God by confessing the Islamic faith statement, many young people easily follow.

Another aspect that draws young people to join Muslim groups is the family feeling in Muslim communities. Muslims stand together like brothers. So once a young man or young woman converts to Islam, he or she will immediately be member of the bigger Muslim family. The individualism of Western societies and the high divorce rate that leads to broken families leaves many people feeling very lonely and starving for close fellowship. What can we do to deal with this? When did you last invite someone in to your home for coffee or to share a meal?

Another characteristic of today's Western societies is that many people's lives are all about making money— either to secure their living or to have fun. Many people just live for themselves and don't see a deeper meaning or purpose in their lives. How many people still live their lives driven by the question of where they will spend eternity, either in heaven or hell? This condition of our society makes it very easy for Muslim groups to win new members by pointing them to a purpose in life. Can we afford to wait for Muslim groups to tell our young generation about the purpose in life?

So we can summarize that there are several issues in the Western societies that we should deal with, if we don't want to wait for Muslim groups to deal with it in their own way.

I hope, my dear reader, that this book will have a fruitful impact on your life. Remember: better than to curse the darkness is to light a candle!

APPENDIX A

MY GOAL IS to make this book as easy to understand as possible even if you know very little about Islam. In this appendix you will learn some important information about Arabic names, quotations from the Quran, and the geography of the Muslim world that will make it easier to understand the terms that are commonly used in this book.

REFERENCES TO MUHAMMAD

There are times when I refer to "the Prophet Muhammad," meaning the founder of Islam. I use the word *prophet* to distinguish him from the many other Muhammads in the Islamic world.

REFERENCES TO THE QURAN

Islam's holy book, the Quran, which is considered the word of Allah, is divided into one hundred fourteen chapters called *surahs*. The surahs are also divided into verses. If you have a copy of the Quran, you can look up passages using the surah and verse numbers. Muslims often refer to the chapters by their chapter name, as the original Quran in Arabic does not contain chapter numbers. The chapter numbers were added later. In this book, however, I have not included the chapter names with every reference because they are of limited significance to the Western reader.

I have used two different English translations of the Quran. One is the version translated by Abdullah Yusef Ali. The other I referred to as *The Noble Quran*. This was published and printed by the king of Saudi Arabia in 1998. This translation expands and clarifies the meaning of the text through comments in parentheses and brackets.

English Translations of the Quran

You should be aware that different English translations of the Quran can render the same verse in very different ways.

For example, Surah 8:39 is a key verse regarding those who reject the Quran, yet the following translation is quite vague:

> And fight them on until there is no more tumult or oppression, and there prevail justice and faith in Allah altogether and everywhere.
> —ALI TRANSLATION

The Noble Quran is a bit more straightforward.

> Fight them until there is no more *Fitnah* (disbelief and polytheism, i.e. worshipping others besides Allah) and the religion (worship) will be for Allah Alone [in the whole of the world].

Reading Arabic Names

I have been told that understanding and reading Arabic names is often difficult for Western readers. Here are a few tips that will help you as you read:

- The words *bin*, *ibn*, and *bn* mean "son of."

- The word *al* means "the."

- When you see a *q*, it is pronounced like the *k* in *kite*.

- When you see two consonants next to each other, the word is pronounced with a very short vowel sound between those consonants. For example, *ibn* would be pronounced "ib-in"; *Qutb* would be pronounced "kutib," in one syllable.

Please see the glossary for a list of commonly referenced names and other key concepts.

THE GEOGRAPHY OF THE MUSLIM WORLD

Western readers are sometimes unfamiliar with the geographic scope of the Muslim world. Although the roots of Islam are in the Arabian peninsula, the Muslim world is much broader.

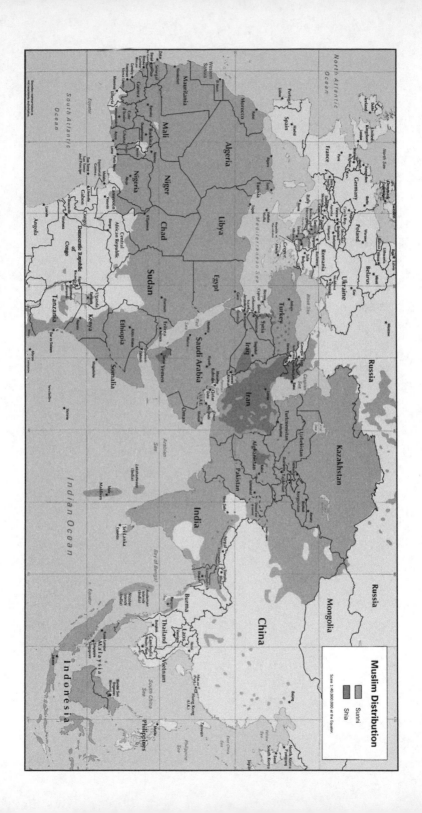

APPENDIX B

THE NAME YOU see on the cover of this book is not the Muslim name that was given to me by my parents in Egypt. However, I would like to say that I have no desire to deceive anyone about my name.

There are some simple reasons why I changed my name—first as a pseudonym for my books and later as my legal name.

Reason #1—For security reasons

After I left Egypt, I spent six years in South Africa, where I became very soon well known. Consequently radical Muslims pursued me diligently, trying to kill me. Several times I was attacked, and it is only by the grace of God that I survived. I had to hide all the time and change my residency from one city to another almost on a monthly basis. Therefore when I wrote my first book in South Africa I decided to publish it under a pseudonym.

Reason #2—For identity reasons

In contrast to Western countries in Egypt you can usually tell by the name whether a person is Muslim or Christian. The name reflects the faith. After I became a Christian I was not comfortable continuing to live by a Muslim name. So when I got baptized it was very normal for me to leave my Muslim identity behind and to choose a Christian name.

Choice of name

I chose the first name of Mark because Mark was a writer of the Gospels. Mark was also the first Christian who went to Egypt with the good news. When Jesus sent the seventy out from Jerusalem, Mark brought the gospel to the city of Alexandria in Egypt.

I chose the last name of Gabriel because this was the surname of the first Christian family with whom I stayed in South Africa after my three months' journey through the continent of Africa. Living with this family was a wonderful experience that made me feel I had become part of the family of Christ.

NOTES

CHAPTER 1: HOW THE ARAB SPRING TURNED TO AN ISIS WINTER

1. Islamonline.net in Arabic, under the page titled "Ask the Expert," under the question that reads, "Mahmoud from Jordan asked, 'What is the meaning of Dar-ul-Islam and Dar-ul-Harb?'"

2. Sayyid Qutb, *Milestones Along the Road* (Delhi: Markazi Maktaba Islami, n.d.), 221.

3. Ibid., 223.

4. Joshua Berlinger, "The Names: Who Has Been Recruited to ISIS From the West," CNN.com, February 26, 2015, http://www.cnn.com/2015/02/25/world/isis-western-recruits/ (accessed June 17, 2015).

5. Hannah Fairfield, Tim Wallace, and Derek Watkins, "How ISIS Expands," *New York Times*, http://www.nytimes.com/interactive/2015/05/21/world/middleeast/how-isis-expands.html (accessed June 17, 2015).

6. The Week, "ISIS: Can the Advance of Islamic State Be Stopped," June 4, 2015, http://www.theweek.co.uk/world-news/isis/59001/isis-who-are-islamic-state-and-can-they-be-stopped#ixzz3dKKzrP4g (accessed June 17, 2015).

CHAPTER 2: FIVE PILLARS OF ISLAMIC RADICALISM

1. "Translation of *Sahih al-Bukhar*," Volume 1, Book 2, Number 36, narrated Abu Huraira, http://www.usc.edu/org/cmje/religious-texts/hadith/bukhari/002-sbt.php (accessed June 18, 2015).

CHAPTER 3: CORE BELIEFS OF ISLAM

1. Akbar S. Ahmed, *Islam Today* (London: I. B. Tauris & Co., 1999), 32–38.

2. Several sources confirm the idea that the verse of the sword had replaced and overridden (*naskh*) the 114 Quranic verses about forgiving the infidels and no longer killing them. These sources include Jalal al-Din al-Syowty, *Ab Bab al-Nuzul [The Reasons for the Revelation]* (Beruit, Lebanon: Dar Eh'yeh al-Alowm [The Signs of Revival House], 1983), vol. 2, p. 37, and Al-Hafz Al Kalbbi, *Al-Tasshel Fi Aleolom Al Tanzel]*.

CHAPTER 5: MISINFORMED BY THE MEDIA

1. Source obtained from the Internet: The transcript of *The Oprah Show* with Queen Rania of Jordan, aired October 10, 2001, as posted at the Oprah.com website on December 23, 2001.
2. *Sahih Al-Bukhari*, vol. 7, book 62, no. 31.
3. Source obtained from the Internet: The transcript of *The Oprah Show* with Queen Rania of Jordan, aired October 10, 2001, as posted at the Oprah.com website on December 23, 2001.
4. Jews believe the Dome of the Rock is built on the site of Solomon's Temple. Islam's holiest site is the Black Stone in Mecca, Saudi Arabia, and its second most holy site is the Mosque of the Prophet, where Muhammad is buried in Medina, Saudi Arabia.

CHAPTER 6: HUMAN RIGHTS UNDER ISLAM

1. "Egypt," Human Rights Watch, http://www.hrw.org/ reports/1995/WR95/MIDEAST-02.htm (accessed June 22, 2015).
2. Farag Foda, *Terrorism* (Cairo, Egypt: Sinai Publishing, n.d.), 13–14.
3. "The Right of Political Asylum for Muslim Apostates in Holland," *Muslim World League Journal*, vol. 1679 (December 8, 2000).
4. Ibid.
5. Ibid.

CHAPTER 8: MUHAMMAD DECLARES JIHAD

1. Ibn Hisham, *The Life of Muhammad*, 3rd edition (Beirut, Lebanon: Dar Al-Jil, 1998), vol. 2, pp. 448, 488; Ibn Kathir, *The Beginning and the End* (Beirut, Lebanon: The Revival of the Arabic Tradition Publishing House, 2001), vol. 22, pp. 100, 207. Ibn Hisham was an Islamic historian.
2. Ibn Hisham, *The Life of Muhammad*, vol. 4, p. 1527.
3. Al Korashi, *Jihad: Another Thought* (Cairo, Egypt: Muktabat Al Haak [The Library of Truth], n.d.).
4. Hisham, *The Life of Muhammad*.
5. A. Guillame, *The Life of Muhammad: A Translation of Ibn Ishq's Sirat Rasul Allah* (Karachi, Pakistan: Oxford University Press, 2003), p. 571.
6. Solomon Basheer, *Tawazn al-Naka-ed [All the Unsimilar Things Are Equal]* (Beirut, Lebanon: Dar al Hari'ah [Freedom House], n.d.), p. 121.

7. Ibn Jarir al-Tabari (838–923), *The History of the Prophet and the Kings*, vol. 5, p. 27.

8. Al-Belezri, *Conquest of the Countries*, vol. 2 (Cairo, Egypt: Dar Al Nahadah [Revival House], 1961), 310.

9. *Al-Nisai*, vol. 3, part 6, page 5, hadith 3,087. Narrated by Abu Hariara. *Al-Nisai* is one of the six correct books of hadith.

10. Ibn Saad, *Al-Tabkat [The Layers]*, vol. 3, 43.

CHAPTER 9: THE ULTIMATE GOAL OF ISLAM

1. Syed Abul A'la Maududi, *Jihad in Islam*, 2nd printing (Delhi 110006, India: Markazi Maktaba Islami, 1973).

2. Ibid.

3. Ibid.

4. Nabil Khalifa, *Lebanon and the Heart of the Islamic Revolution* (Beirut, 1984), 93, 120.

CHAPTER 11: WHEN LIES ARE JUSTIFIED

1. The Shafi'i historian Ibn Kathir, in the events of the year 1293–1294, tells of the affair of 'Assaf al-Nasrani (the Christian), who was reported by witnesses to have cursed the Prophet. Ibn Taymiyah and a companion, al-Faraqi, apparently implicated in the affair for encouraging the assault and battery to which 'Assaf and his Bendoin protector were victims, were flogged and placed under house arrest. This was the episode behind Ibn Taymiyah's work *Kitab al-scrim al-maslul 'ala shatim al-rasul (The Sharp Sword Drawn Against the Revilor of the Messenger [of God])*.

2. Ibn al-Kayim, *Al taib Wal Khabith [The Pure and the Unpure]* (Beirut, Lebanon: Dar al-Al [House of Knowledge], n.d.), 199.

3. Kathir, *The Beginning and the End*.

4. Ibid.

5. Egyptian president's national address after the first day of the Iraqi invasion of Kuwait.

6. Abi Hamid al-Ghazali, *Ehia Al-owlom Al-Den [A Revival of the Religious Books]* (Cairo, Egypt: Maktabet al-Turas, 1971), 3, 137.

7. The Quran refers to this incident in Surah 24:11, which speaks of "those who brought forth the slander."

8. Sahih Al-Bukhari, 9-vol. set, English translation by Muhsin Khan (Cairo, Egypt: Dar Ah'ya Us-sunnah), vol. 8, book 82, no. 805.

CHAPTER 12: MUHAMMAD'S USE OF MOSQUES

1. "U.S. Bombs Hit Mosque, Kills 15 Worshippers," Lebanon News Center at www.lebanon-guide.com (accessed October 24, 2001).

2. William Branigin and Rajiv Ch, and rasekaran, "Informants Enable a Deadly Raid," *Washington Post*, October 25, 2001, http://www.washingtonpost.com/archive/politics/2001/10/25/informants-enable-a-deadly-raid/87435a49-8408-46f0-84ce-760bc564ef41/ (accessed June 22, 2015).

3. Mahmoud Fouzi, *Abed Al-Halim Mousa [Secrets of the Resignation of Mohammed]*, 2nd ed. (Cairo, Egypt: Maktabat Al Hiyat [Library of Life], n.d.), 40.

CHAPTER 13: FOREFATHERS OF TERRORISM

1. Hisham, *The Life of Muhammad*.

2. *Sahih Al-Bukhari*, volume titled Book of Jihad, vol. 4, book 52, page 34 and following.

3. Shahrstanni, *Religion and Sects* (Beirut, Lebanon: Dar As Sarool [House of Happiness], 1949), 114, and Aby-El-Hassan Al-Ashri, Islamic Articles, vol. 1, 88.

CHAPTER 14: THE FOUNDING FATHER OF MODERN JIHAD

1. Adel Hamooda, *Sayyid Qutb: From the Village to the Gallows* (Cairo, Egypt: Sinai Publishing, 1987), pp. 92–94.

2. To my amazement, the English translation of one of Sayyid Qutb's books, *Social Justice in Islam*, is actually available at Amazon.com.

3. Sayyid Qutb, *Ma'alim fi el-Tareek [Signs Along the Road]* as quoted in Hamooda, *Sayyid Qutb*.

4. Ibid., 10.

5. Ibid., 22.

6. Ibid.

7. Ibid.

CHAPTER 15: THE PHILOSOPHERS OF JIHAD

1. As quoted in Salah Serea, "Clips of Message of Faith," *El-Yakaza El-Arabeya [Arabic Revival Magazine]* (December 1986).

2. Ibid.

3. Ibid.

4. Shokri Moustafa, *El-Tawaseemat [Expectation]* (Cairo, Egypt: Shorouk International, n.d.).

5. *Rose El-Yousef Magazine*, published in Cairo, Egypt (July 11, 1977): 6.

6. Shokri Moustafa, *Al-Kalafa [The Leader]* (Cairo, Egypt: Shorouk International, n.d.).

CHAPTER 18: TREACHERY BETWEEN TERRORISTS

1. Adel Hamooda, *Bombs and the Quran*, 3rd ed. (Cairo, Egypt: Sinai Publishing, 1989), p. 44.

2. That committee included Mohammed Abdul-Salam Farag, Abod Al-Zomor, Karim Zohdi, Najeh Ibrahim, Fouad Al-Dolabi, Ali Sharif, Essam Dirbala, Assim Abdul-Majed, Hamdi Abdul Rahman, and Talat Qusam.

3. Following are the regions and their leaders: Cairo and Al-Giza region, Mohammed Abdul-Salam Farag; Al Minya region, Essam Dirbala and Fouad Al-Dolabi; Asyut region, Assim Abdul-Majed, Osama Hafez and Najeh Ibrahim; Quna and Nagh Hamadi regions, Ali Sharif and Talat Qusam.

CHAPTER 20: JUSTICE LOSES, QURAN WINS

1. Mahmoud Faouzi, *Omar Abdul Rachman: The American Sheikh Is Coming* (Cairo, Egypt: Dar Al aaten, 1993), 26–39.

CHAPTER 21: JIHAD BLEEDS OUT OF EGYPT

1. *Sahih al-Bukhari.*

CHAPTER 22: NEW STRATEGY: ATTACK THE WEST

1. I received this information from a video produced by the United States Coptic Church association. The Coptic Church is the largest Christian denomination in Egypt. If you want more details, contact the director of the US Copts association—Mike@copts.com.

GLOSSARY

Abbas al-Madani—leader and official spokesman of the Algerian Islamic Salvation Front

Ahmed Yassin—spiritual leader of the Palestinian Hamas

Al-Azhar University—oldest Islamic university in the world; spiritual authority of Islam located in Cairo, Egypt

al-Gama'a al-Islamiyya—the Islamic Group (IG); emerged during the 1970s mainly in Egyptian jails and later on in some of the Egyptian universities

al-Husayn—son of Ali ibn Abi Talib, grandson of Muhammad

Ali Belhadj—popular Algerian preacher who also served in leadership with the Algerian Islamic Salvation Front

Ali ibn Abi Talib—first cousin of Muhammad and one of his earliest converts; fourth caliph, selected as caliph after the murder of Uthman; one of the Righteous Caliphs

al-Jihad—radical fundamentalist group established in Egypt that spread to many Muslim countries, such as Palestine and others

Allah—the God of Islam

al Qaeda—fundamentalist Islamic organization founded by Osama bin Laden and now led by Ayman al-Zawahiri

Anwar al-Sadat—former president of Egypt; assassinated by radical Muslim fundamentalists on October 6, 1981

Ayatollah Ruhollah Khomeini—chief Islamic leader of Iran from 1979 to 1989; returned to Iran in 1979 from exile in France after the shah fled Iran

Ayman al-Zawahiri—leader of the al-Jihad; al Qaeda leader; on FBI's Most Wanted Terrorist list

Battle of Badr—First battle of Muhammad in which he defeated his rivals from Mecca at the Valley of Badr

Caliph—title given to those who succeeded the prophet Muhammad as real or nominal ruler of the Muslim world, with all his powers except that of prophecy; from the Arabic word *khalifa*, literally meaning "one who replaces someone else who left or died"

el Kharij—seventh-century Islamic movement calling for return to purity of faith

fatwa—legal opinion

Gamal Abdel Nasser—president of Egypt, 1956–1970

George Habash—leader of the Popular Front for the Liberation of Palestine

hadith—the reported sayings and actions of Muhammad recorded in six sets of books also known as *Sunnah*

Hamas—Islamic Resistance Movement located in Palestine

Hasan al-Turabi—leader of the Sudanese fundamentalist Islamic organization al-Islamia

Hassan al-Banna—founder and first leader of the Muslim Brotherhood Movement; assassinated by Egyptian police in 1949

Hassan Nasrallah—Hizbollah leader

hijab—a woman's veil or head scarf

Hizbollah (also Hezbollah)—"Party of God"; Lebanese Islamic party

Hosni Mubarak—Egyptian president from 1981–2011; assumed office after the assassination of Anwar al-Sadat

Ibn Hisham—early Islamic historian

Ibn Taymiyah—thirteenth- and fourteenth-century scholar who called for a return to the ways of the "pious ancestors" (*al-salaf al-salih*)

imam—an Islamic leader; usually in charge of a mosque

infidel—one who rejects the teachings of Islam

Islamic Salvation Front (FIS)—North Africa's first legal Islamic political party, first recognized by Algeria's government in 1988; later split into a moderate group and a more militant wing called the Islamic Salvation Army

Jamaat-i-Islami (Islamic Society)—fundamentalist Islamic organization of Pakistan

jihad—holy war; fighting those who resist Islam

jizyah—tax that must be paid by anyone who chooses to keep their own faith and not convert to Islam

Khaled al-Islambouli—one of the convicted assassins of Egyptian president Anwar al-Sadat

Mahmoud Nokrashy Pasha—premier of Egypt assassinated by Muslim Brotherhood on December 28, 1948

Mawlana Abul Ala Mawdudi—leader of the Jamaat-i-Islami of Pakistan

Mecca—birthplace of Muhammad and place where he first received Quranic verses from the angel Gabriel; located in present-day Saudi Arabia

Medina—originally called Yathrib; name of city was changed to Medina ("the Prophet's city") after Muhammad relocated there; located in present-day Saudi Arabia

Muammar Qaddafi—Libyan leader

Muawiya ibn Abi Sufyan—governor of Syria who opposed the selection of Ali as caliph after the murder of Uthman

Muhammad ibn Abd al-Wahhab—founder of the eighteenth century puritanical Wahhabi movement

Muhammad Reza Shah Pahlavi—shah of Iran at the time of the revolution led by Ayatollah Khomeini in 1979

Muhammad—Arab prophet and founder of Islam, born AD 570; the Westernized spelling is Mohammed

Muslim Brotherhood—Islamic organization encompassing several nations and Islamic groups

Mustafa Kemal Ataturk—Turkish leader who abolished the Ottoman/Turkish caliphate system in 1922

Naguib Mahfouz—winner of the 1988 Nobel Prize for Literature; stabbed outside his home in Cairo in 1994

naskh—system of Quranic interpretation where new verses override previous verses

Omar Abdel Rahman—former leader of al-Jihad in Egypt, currently imprisoned in the United States for his involvement in the 1993 World Trade Center bombing

Osama bin Laden—suspected mastermind of the September 11, 2001 terrorist attacks against the United States; former leader of al Qaeda; killed by US forces on May 2, 2011

People of the Book—Jews and Christians, so named in the Quran

Popular Front for the Liberation of Palestine—progressive working-class party of Palestine, guided by Marxism and Leninism

Quran—the Islamic holy book

Quraysh—powerful governing tribe of Mecca at the time of Muhammad's birth; Muhammad's father, a trader named Abdullah, was a member of this tribe

Ramadan—the ninth month of the Muslim calendar, during which a daily fast is observed from dawn until sunset

Saddam Hussein—Iraqi political leader, president of Iraq 1979–2003

Salman Rushdie—Writer of *The Satanic Verses,* which caused the Ayatollah Khomeini to issue a *fatwa* sanctioning his death

Sayyid Qutb—Egyptian author and philosopher whose writings were banned by Egyptian government; he was arrested and sentenced to death in 1965 and executed in 1966

Sharia—Islamic law regarding the duties of Muslims toward Allah presented by Quran and hadith

sheikh—term of reverence for an ordained religious leader in Islam

Shiite—Islamic sect; followers of Ali ibn Abi Talib as the successor of Muhammad

Shokri Ahmad Moustafa—popular Islamic movement leader in Egypt; executed by the government in 1977

Sunni—Islamic sect; followers of Umar ibn al-Khattab as the successor of Muhammad

Surah—a chapter of the Quran

Taliban—Islamic fundamentalist group of Afghanistan

Uhud—hill where famous battle was fought by Muhammad and his new converts against Arabs who rejected the call of Islam

Umar ibn al-Khattab—second caliph assassinated in AD 644 by a Persian slave bent on avenging the conquest of his people

Uthman ibn Affan—third successor of Islam

Wahhabi—eighteenth-century puritanical movement that in time became the official creed of the Saudi dynasty; adherents observed literalism and strict observance of Muslim rituals

Yasser Arafat—chairman of the Palestine Liberation Organization (PLO) until his death in 2004

Yathrib—ancient name of the city of Medina; name changed to Medina ("the Prophet's city") after Muhammad relocated there

Yazid—son of Muawiya ibn Abi Sufyan

BIBLIOGRAPHY

Books Published in Arabic

Abdul-Majed, Assim and Najeh Ibrahim. *The Constitution of the Islamic Jihad*. Cairo, Egypt: Al Jemaah al-Islamiya, 1984. (The authors wrote this book while in prison.)

Al-Banna, Hassan. *Wednesday Dialogue*. Cairo, Egypt: Manshurat ad-Dawa [Literature of Evangelism], 1979.

Al-Masry, Ebn Eyas. *Al-Nejum Al-Zaharah [The Bright Stars]*. Cairo, Egypt: Dar al Nahadah [House of Revival], 1972.

Al-Nadawy, Abu al-Hasan. *The Struggle Between Eastern and Western Ideology*. Lucknow, India: Academy of Islamic Research, 1977.

Al-Salem, Mohammed Abed. *Al-Fareda Al-Gaaba [The Missing Commitments]*. Cairo, Egypt: Tanzim al-Jihad [The Jihad Movement], 1979.

Al-Tobari, Ebn Garir. *The History of the Prophet and the Kings*. Beirut, Lebanon: Dar al-Fiq [House of Thought], 1987. (This is the oldest Islamic history book.)

Commentaries on the Quran written by the following authors: Al-Alussi, Ibn Kathir, Al-Zamakshary, Al-Bidawy. All published by Almoktar al-Islami in Cairo, Egypt.

El-Rahman, Aisha Abd. *The Wives of the Prophet*. Morocco: Dar El Hilal, 1971.

Foda, Farag. *Terrorism*. Cairo, Egypt: Sinai Publishing, n.d.

The Hadith (six series of books) published by Almoktar
        al-Islami, Cairo, Egypt. The authors of these book
        series include: Sahih al-Bukhari and al-Korashi.

Hamooda, Adel. *Sayyid Qutb: From the Village to the
        Gallows.* Cairo, Egypt: Sinai Publishing, 1987.
        (Hamooda is an Egyptian author who specializes
        in books about Islamic terrorism.)

———. *The Road to Violence* (a book about Shokri
        Moustafa). Cairo, Egypt: Sinai Publishing, 1987.

———. *Bombs and the Quran: The Story of Jihad
        Fundamentalist Groups.* Cairo, Egypt: Sinai
        Publishing, 1989.

Huwaody, Fahmi. *Hata la-Takon-Fitnah [Preventing
        Conflict],* 2nd ed. Cairo, Egypt: Dar el-Shorouk,
        1989.

Ibn Taymiyah. *The Greatest Fatwa.* Beirut, Lebanon: Dar
        al Qutub [House of Books], 1987.

Imara, Mohammed. *Mawdudi and the Islamic Revival.*
        Cairo, Egypt: Dar el-Shorouk, 1987.

Mawdudi, Mawlana Abul Ala. *The Islamic Government.*
        Cairo, Egypt, 1980.

Moustafa, Shokri. *Al-Kalafa [The Leader].* Cairo, Egypt:
        Al-Takfir Wal-Hijra [Come Out From the
        Apostates], n.d.

Qutb, Sayyid. *In the Shadow of the Quran* (a commentary
        on the Quran). Cairo, Egypt and Beirut, Lebanon:
        Dar el-Shorouk International, n.d.

———. *Signs Along the Road.* Cairo, Egypt and Beirut,
        Lebanon: Dar el-Shorouk International, n.d.

———. *This Religion.* Cairo, Egypt and Beirut, Lebanon: Dar
        el-Shorouk International, n.d.

———. *Social Justice in Islam*. Cairo, Egypt and Beirut, Lebanon: Dar el-Shorouk International, n.d.

———. *The Picture of Arts in the Quran*. Cairo, Egypt and Beirut, Lebanon: Dar el-Shorouk International, n.d.

———. *Our War With the Jews*. Cairo, Egypt and Beirut, Lebanon: Dar el-Shorouk International, n.d.

———. *The Future of This Religion*. Cairo, Egypt and Beirut, Lebanon: Dar el-Shorouk International, n.d.

———. *Establishing Islamic Society*. Cairo, Egypt and Beirut, Lebanon: Dar el-Shorouk International, n.d.

Serea, Salah. *El-Tawaseemat [Expectation]*. Cairo, Egypt: self-published by Salah Serea, 1973.

Shalaby, Ahmed. *The Islamic Encyclopedia*, Cairo edition. Cairo, Egypt: Dar al-Nahada [House of Revival], 1982.

———. *The Encyclopedia of Islamic Civilization*, Cairo edition. Cairo, Egypt: Dar al-Nahada [House of Revival], 1982.

———. *Islam and the World*. Cairo, Egypt: Dar al-Nahada [House of Revival].

———. *The War in Kuwait*. Cairo, Egypt: Dar al-Nahada [House of Revival].

———. *The Jews in Darkness*. Cairo, Egypt: Dar al-Nahada [House of Revival].

Books Published in English

Arnold, Thomas. *The Preaching of Islam*. Columbia, MO: South Asia Books, 1990.

———. *The Caliphate*. New York: Oxford Press, 2000.

Bodansky, Yossef. *Target America: Terrorism in the USA Today.* New York: S.P.I. Books/Shapolsky Publishers, Inc., 1993.

Emerton, Ephraim. *Medieval Europe.* Bowling Green, NY: Gordon Press, a division of Krishna Press, 1976.

Hitti, Philip. *The Arabs: A Short History.* Washington, DC: Regnery Publishing, Inc., 1996.

Huntington, Samuel. *The Clash of Civilizations and the Remaking of World Order.* Touchstone Books, 1998.

Nixon, Richard. *Seize the Moment: America's Challenge in a One-Superpower World.* New York: Simon and Schuster, 1992.

Sarton, George. *A History of Science.* New York: Norton and Company, 1952.

RECOMMENDED READING

Morey, Robert A. *Islamic Invasion.* Las Vegas, NV: Christian Scholar's Press, 2001.

———. *Winning the War Against Radical Islam.* Las Vegas, NV: Christian Scholar's Press, 2002.

Shorrosh, A. *Islam Revealed.* Nashville, TN: Thomas Nelson, 1988.

OTHER BOOKS BY THE AUTHOR

Islam and the Jews
(FrontLine, 2003)
Find out the role of Islam in the clash between Israel
and the Muslim world. It exposes what the Quran
and Muhammad taught about Jewish people.

Jesus and Muhammad
(FrontLine, 2004)
Look at the profound differences and surprising parallels
between the lives and teachings of Jesus and Muhammad.

Journey Into the Mind of an Islamic Terrorist
(FrontLine, 2006)
Get inside the mind of an Islamic terrorist. This book exposes the frightening
logic behind Islamic radical groups.

Culture Clash
(FrontLine, 2007)
Discover what it would be like to live under Islamic
law in this eye-opening exposé of the difference
between Islamic culture and modern culture.

Coffee With the Prophet
(Gabriel Publishing, 2008)
Learn about Islamic history and culture
through a novel that envisions how Muhammad
would behave in the modern world.

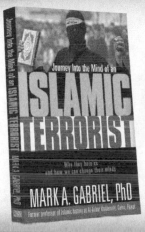